STEPPING INTO DARKNESS

A journey across Mozambique,
following the mighty Zambezi River

ALASDAIR CAMPBELL

www.newgeneration-publishing.com

 New Generation Publishing

Contents

If you want to travel quickly, go alone.
If you want to go far, go together.

African proverb

Prologue

The first punch caught me in the side of the face, just below the cheek bone. I had expected to be hit, but it shocked me all the same. It was a punch delivered with force, with meaning, and further blows to the head followed. Some sharp kicks down my sides caused me to wince in pain.

'Behave yourselves!' I shouted, more out of annoyance than fear, but I knew the situation was rapidly getting out of control.

I would have tried to block the blows, except they had now bound my hands tightly behind me with twine. My feet had also been tied together with my own belt so I could offer little resistance. Someone rifled in my thigh pockets and I felt my phone being removed. A few more punches were thrown and my head rocked from side to side with the impact. I could taste blood in my mouth and wondered if their blows had dislodged a tooth.

'I'm a tourist! A tourist!' I shouted, but my pleas were met with further strikes.

The multitude of legs in my vision told me a larger crowd had gathered and I looked around anxiously for someone in authority, perhaps even the 'Mfumu' of the village. I had learnt that every village was led by one and that I should ask for them if I ever needed help.

'Is the Mfumu here?' I asked anxiously of those nearest me.

I knew that everyone who could hear me knew what the term meant, but my question was met with indifference. I asked again, louder this time, but no one stepped forward to help. Just then, as I was still on the ground, I felt two hands grab my head and pull it violently back and then to each side, then so hard upwards that I thought the intention was to remove it from my body. I shouted out in pain and anger again, wondering what I had done to be treated so badly.

Then the two men standing closest to me grabbed an arm

each and bustled me along the track, which I presumed was back towards the main settlement. Small children and teenagers running alongside began laughing and shouting, offering taunts and although I couldn't understand what they were saying, I was clearly in the middle of a mob that had plans for me. As the men dragged me, I felt one of my shoes slip off and a little further on the other followed. We made limited progress, as my feet were bound and the two captors became annoyed and began to pull me along faster, my socks scraping through the sandy soil. In my confused state, I imagined the strange twisting line in the dirt that would mystify passers-by.

After a few hundred metres, the man on my right, who was weaker than his friend, let go of my arm with a gasp and slipped behind me. His companion, a lean, strong man of medium height, jerked me forward with renewed vigour, his heavy breathing resounding in my ears. A woman, who had been shouting from the sidelines, rushed forward, took hold of the vacated limb with relish and assisted in pulling me along, hurling hysterical abuse in my direction. Catching a whiff of her scent, which was almost unhuman, I almost gagged. At times, when our progress slackened, she gripped my arm tighter, as if possessed by demons, forcing us forward. I kept shouting 'Tourist! Tourist!' but the crowd had already decided who I was and what was to come.

Eventually, we moved off the path towards some huts and into what looked like the centre of the village. In a snatched glance, I saw that the dwellings were basic with medium-sized logs as the walls and simple thatch for a roof, a design probably unchanged since the time of early explorers to the region. The ground was flattened down hard from the many feet over the years and I could see a large mound of ash denoting a fire for the huts, straight in front of me.

I was forced onto my knees without ceremony and the children, who had quietened coming into the settlement, found their voice again and began jeering and shouting in earnest. The crowd, old and young and close to a hundred people by now, formed a daunting circle around me, the closest an arm's length away.

A man close to me pushed through the crowd, over to the mound of ash, scooped up a handful and walked purposefully back towards me. He then deposited the powdery matter onto my head, rubbing it vigorously into my hair and I could feel it falling down my face and into my eyes.

'Mfumu! Mfumu!' I shouted again, wanting the leader of the village to appear, calm everything down and make the nightmare disappear. But all I saw was a sea of dark faces, shouting, jeering and showing hostility. I flexed my throbbing fingers behind me which had been stamped on during the scuffle.

The crowd pressed closer and I was hit hard with a fist in the back of the head several times. Then, a man, probably in his thirties, grabbed my arm, shouted at the crowd and with the assistance of someone else, pulled me roughly to another spot a short distance away. A few of the women began angrily pointing at me and yelling hysterically. I couldn't believe that I was the cause of such anger. My unlikely saviour shouted back in equal measure, gesturing wildly, but the women didn't stop.

An old plastic chair was dragged along the ground and I was pushed down into the seat. My hands and feet were still bound, but it was good to sit and take the strain off my knees. I was still getting punches to the back of the head, but they were just annoying and not causing me damage.

A woman pushed through the mob and tapped the arm of one of the older men standing in front of me. In her hands was an iron, one of those heavy, old cast iron affairs that you still see in industrial era museums.

'Jesus Christ!' I muttered under my breath, fixated on the object.

The man glanced down at her, paused for what seemed an age and slowly shook his head, before she reluctantly withdrew. The implement she was carrying was clearly meant to do me harm and my mind raced with the terrible possibilities.

Minutes later, a young man appeared and told me in broken English that he was a teacher, asking why I was there. I quickly explained that I was heading for Chinde and the coast. He requested to see my papers and I told him they were in my pack, which I hadn't seen since being jumped on. The man looked around nervously, and I asked him to fetch the police as a matter of urgency.

'It is very bad what they are doing, but it is out of my hands. They will do what they need to do,' he replied hopelessly, glancing away.

I asked him as calmly as I could what the problem was and why I had been so badly mistreated. The man paused before answering, staring into my eyes.

'They think you are a vampire!' he replied.

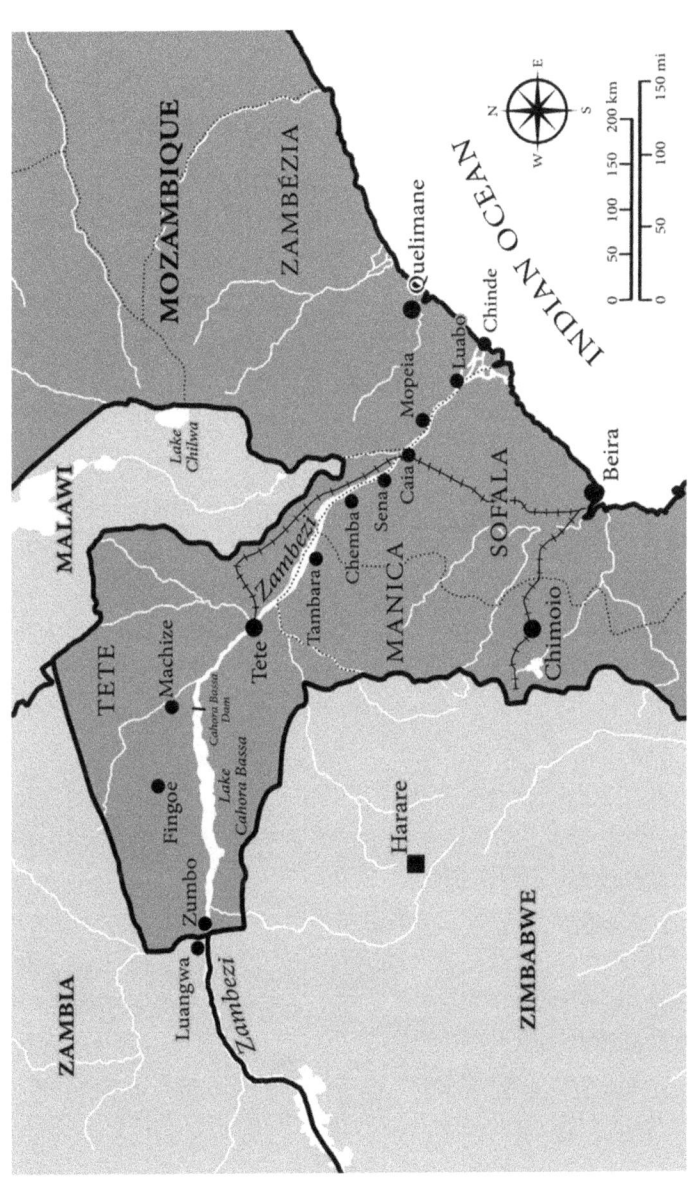

Chapter One - Zumbo

Crossing the Luangwa River and then joining the Zambezi into Mozambique by simple craft felt like sailing back in time. Fishermen in older boats than ours were casting their flimsy nets into the murky water, hoping for a catch, whilst women on the sandy beach vigorously washed their clothes. It was a cool and overcast August morning, which felt strange as it had been baking hot at a similar time in the days previous.

I was travelling with Chaz Powell, who the year before in 2016, had attempted to be the first person to walk the length of the Zambezi River in one push. Although he had followed its course through Zambia, he had failed to make it into Mozambique due to election riots in some of the towns on its banks. I had followed his journey with interest and contacted him afterwards to see if he wanted a companion to finish the trip. After hearing about some of my own expeditions, he had readily agreed and we began to plan the trip together.

My own motivations revolved around wanting to do something unique and testing in the continent that I loved most: Africa. I had travelled to many of its wonderful countries, but had rarely been to an area so seldom visited by tourists. I knew that people jetted into the beaches and dive spots on Mozambique's coast, but few made it inland and even fewer explored the Zambezi River and the Cahora Bassa Lake that it flowed through. It was a country that I knew little about, but I researched it extensively in the lead up to the journey. I was interested to see how the people of Mozambique were coping with their daily lives, having emerged from a brutal civil war in the early 1990s.

In my experience, each of the nations on the African continent had their own unique sights, climates, wildlife and cultures and I was sure that Mozambique would have similar allure. The expedition would be demanding, as we would be trekking large distances every day in high temperatures and for the most part living rough. When planning the trip, I was interested to read a book by George Martelli, who had studied and written about David Livingstone's expedition along the Zambezi in the 1850s. In it, he described the great explorer's thoughts on what could also lay ahead for us:

'He himself would describe the hardships of African travel – sleeping on the ground, living off a diet of manioc or millet meal, interminable marching under a tropical sun, frequent soakings from wading through swamps or streams, repeated attacks of malaria or dysentery, not to mention the constant risking of life or limb – as daunting only to those who were fastidious over trifles.' (2)

Another reason for undertaking the trip was to forge another direction in my life, after serving as an army officer and then as a headhunter for high profile companies around the globe. As a soldier, I had served in some interesting spots, picking up useful skills and firing my thirst for travel off the beaten track. As a headhunter, I had been attracted to the Arabian Gulf as a region of interest to explore. After five years working there and passing fifty, I was bored, cynical and frustrated and decided to leave, wanting to do something different. I was financially secure and, not relishing the prospect of returning to chilly England, decided to travel and write, and base myself close to the Mediterranean Sea, where I could live life at my own pace and in countries that didn't take themselves too seriously.

In preparation for this adventure, Chaz and I had met several times to discuss the journey and how we should go about it. The route was simple enough; we would follow the course of the Zambezi River from its most westerly point of Zumbo in Mozambique and use the river as a handrail all the way to the town of Chinde on the Indian Ocean, well over eight hundred kilometres away. The Zambezi is the fourth longest river in Africa, known as the 'Great River' by some tribes that live along its banks, with its source in the north west of Zambia, close to the border with the Democratic Republic of Congo (DRC). Stretching for over two and a half thousand kilometres, it flows into Angola, sweeps back into Zambia, touches Namibia and Botswana, before running along the border with Zimbabwe and finally entering Mozambique and on towards the sea.

The Zambezi region was known to medieval geographers as the Empire of Monomotapa and the course of the river, its tributaries and the lakes along its route were broadly accurate on maps of the time. It is thought that much of the information used to construct the early maps came from Arab slavers who had penetrated far into the heart of Africa. The first European to visit the inland Zambezi River was the Portuguese explorer Antonio Fernandes in 1511, with the objective of reporting on commercial conditions and activities in that part of the continent. Centuries later, Dr David Livingstone led the first exploration of the upper Zambezi and it was whilst following its course to the sea that he discovered the Victoria Falls in 1855.

I had studied satellite maps extensively, particularly along the Cahora Bassa Lake and around Tete, the Zambezi delta and Chinde itself. For hours I had studied tracks in the dirt, and where they went, from five hundred kilometres above the earth and had built up a good understanding of the lay of the land. I knew that when my boots hit the real dirt, however, those tracks would look very different.

We would travel light, carrying only daysacks weighing about ten kilos, minimal gear and dry rations to be replenished along the way and we aimed to walk around thirty kilometres a day. My companion, from his Zambia experience, assured me that we would also be able to supplement our diet with chickens, fish and fruit bought from the locals on our journey. We would carry a few litres of water in our packs to keep us hydrated, and would top up from wells and the river itself, using specialised filter bottles.

My trekking companion had made some contacts along the Cahora Bassa Lake, where we hoped for the occasional stay in lodges, but when we were out in the wild we would camp using lightweight tents and sleeping mats. He had assured me that sleeping bags would not be needed as it would be hot and so we both took Thermolite liners to help ward off the chill.

The year before, Chaz had sought advice from another adventurer called David Lemon, a seventy-year-old former policeman, originally from Zimbabwe who had walked the length of the Zambezi, completing it in 2014. He had to make the journey in several stages – he suffered severe weight loss along the way, and caught malaria three times – over a couple of years. It was still a remarkable feat for someone of his age and although he had porters to carry his pack along the way, he was clearly as tough as old boots. David had provided useful information about the river and his book *In Livingstone's Footsteps* gave me a good overview of what to expect.

As someone who keeps himself fit and ran most evenings in the Gulf, I was in pretty good shape but knew that I needed to do some long distance walking to get used to carrying a pack again. Chaz would do his own physical preparation by undertaking long walks in the wild near his Midlands home. In May, a few months before departing for Zambia, the start point of the expedition, I chose to walk the Camino De Santiago, a pilgrimage route from Saint-Jean-Pied-de-Port in southern France across the north of Spain to Santiago de Compostela. It is a distance of over eight hundred kilometres, a trip I had always wanted to take but never had the time. Although I am not religious, I found it to be a spiritual journey with plenty of time to think, reflect on one's experiences and enjoy the company of fellow pilgrims. It was also the perfect opportunity to get walking fit, break in my shoes and test the rest of my gear. Walking over thirty kilometres a day, I completed it in twenty-six days and, apart from a few blisters, I had no problems. A month later, tanned and slim from my sojourn in Spain, I flew to Livingstone in Zambia to meet up with Chaz and make the final preparations for the expedition. After a week discussing the route in fine detail, organising supplies and a stopover in the capital

Lusaka to organise visas, we began to trek towards the Mozambican border.

Luangwa is the most south-easterly point of Zambia and the stepping stone into Mozambique. We had arrived there dusty and tired after walking around the Lower Zambezi National Park, and hoped to find somewhere to stay before heading across the border.

Wandering over to what looked like a reasonable lodge, set back from the river, protected by a high wall and nestled in the trees, we asked if we could stay but were told that it was some kind of civil service retreat and therefore unable to accept travellers. They could, however, sell us something to eat and we settled down in the shade to enjoy a hot chicken and rice lunch, the best food we had tasted in days.

We set off into town to try to find a kindly lodge owner who would put us up for the night. On our trek across Zambia, Chaz had told me about the hospitality he had received along the Zambezi the year before, being given rooms and food and we were hoping to tap into that generosity. On our way, we passed a huge baobab tree by the side of the road, which I had read about as being the site of a former slave market, in use right up until the late 1800s. Apparently, huge chains were wrapped around the trunk which the unfortunates were manacled to.

After a few attempts, trekking up and down the hills of the town in the heat of the afternoon, we had been given cold water and sympathetic smiles but no offers of free board. We realised that our luck wasn't in and so retreated to a roadside restaurant to discuss our options in the shade.

Once known as Feira, Luangwa is the oldest settlement in Zambia, where it became an infamous hub for the Arab slave trade. The wretched human cargo, having been taken from inland Africa, was shipped along the Zambezi River and then sent to the slave markets along the coast. The trade lasted from the mid-1700s until the end of the eighteenth century. A memorial stone by the water stated that there were records of a fifteenth century settlement there, abandoned a hundred years later. The Portuguese, looking to establish a trading base in the area, brought the place back to life in 1745, when they began to build a church and houses for its soldiers.

There followed a period of fights with local tribes and general instability and the settlement was again abandoned in 1830, with the Portuguese moving east along the Zambezi to safer territory. In 1856, David Livingstone passed through on his Zambezi expedition, a year after discovering the Victoria Falls in present-day Zambia. He described the place as derelict and found the remains of the original bell near the shell of the church. In 1887, John Harrison Clark, one of the first District Governors, set up his headquarters in Feira and controlled the area around the town for many years. It became a staging post for the movement of cattle from Tanganyika (now Tanzania) to Rhodesia (now Zimbabwe), but its relevance slowly died as roads and railways began to stretch across the region.

The town's location is strategically important though, being at the confluence of the Luangwa and Zambezi rivers and the borders with Mozambique and Zimbabwe. It has only one road in and out, which connects to the Great East Road a hundred kilometres north, and there are no bridges to the neighbouring countries. Luangwa had an end of the line feel about it, but that's probably how the locals liked it.

The owner of the restaurant where we sat mentioned a place where we could get a room. After a few cold drinks we headed for it, wondering what we would find. We crossed over the road and passed the small market. The main items on offer were what looked like secondhand clothes, which I guessed had arrived in the country from charities many thousands of miles away, but were now for sale. Also available to buy were cheap sports bags, plastic shoes, batteries and bins, but there were few takers.

After walking through back alleys and into dead ends and asking locals where to find the place we had been told about, we eventually spotted a scruffy sign and stumbled into a compound. The receptionist of the Nyabota Lodge seemed surprised to see us, but he quoted a reasonable rate for the room and we headed for it, glad to be out of the afternoon heat. It was a simple affair: two beds, large holes in the window netting, a bathroom and shower with running water. What was also included, at no extra charge, was a squadron of mosquitoes that would swoop down on us as it got dark, keeping up their attacks until dawn.

As the light began to fade, I left my friend to rest in the room and wandered the kilometre down to the river beach where boats were moored. I wanted to have a look at the country that we would enter the following morning. Where I stood, there were streetlights behind me and I could hear the occasional car or motorbike passing by, but on the other side of the river there was only darkness, as if it was empty of life. It was like looking into another world. From my research, I knew that Mozambique was an impoverished country with a troubled past. I didn't know how the population would receive my companion and I as we journeyed along the Zambezi.

For months, I had been looking forward to this moment and felt excitement about exploring a new country, where few travellers visited, but I also felt a little wary and unsure. We both knew about the threat from landmines, sprinkled around the country like confetti during the civil war, and had agreed to stick to paths where possible. We also knew that we might come across snakes, crocodiles and other creatures, but we assumed people would probably pose the greatest threat. Trekking across Zambia to get here, a rapidly developing country, we had been met with kindness and generosity from the locals. Mozambique was a different matter though; we knew that where there's poverty, crime usually follows in its wake.

Standing there, staring into darkness, it seemed so long ago that we had been in Livingstone in Zambia, making the final preparations for the journey. The town was named after the explorer, who had been the first European to discover the Victoria Falls, some ten kilometres away. It was quite a modern looking place, with heavy traffic passing through and had a young, vibrant feel to it. We had stayed for a week at the wonderful Fawlty Towers Backpacker Lodge on the south side of town, camping on the lawn and enjoying the company of fellow travellers, many of whom were overlanding across Africa.

After breakfast each day, we would pore over paper maps and the Sygic app on our iPhones, which provided simple mapping without the need of the internet. Chaz also viewed his basic satnav device, which provided another level of detail. Using all the tools at our disposal, we discussed the route over and over and what we might find in the country. My companion also reached out to his contacts in Mozambique to gain up to date advice and to try to secure accommodation for the first few days of our trip.

In a quiet period, I took the opportunity to visit the Livingstone museum in the town, which apart from showing the flora and fauna we might encounter on our journey, also had a section dedicated to the explorer, showing some of his equipment and maps from his Zambezi expedition. I had smiled when I studied pictures of him leading his companions and porters, laden down with trunks and supplies through savannah and swamp, knowing that soon I would be following in their footsteps carrying just a small 35 litre pack.

On one of the days towards the end of my stay in Livingstone, I took a bus down to see the Victoria Falls. Walking along a path through dense scrub, the sound of cascading water began to build until it suddenly appeared in front of me. Stretching almost two kilometres into the distance, with a drop of over a hundred metres, it is classified as the world's largest waterfall, based on the volume of water from the Zambezi River passing over it. Also known as 'The Smoke that Thunders' by the Kololo tribe who live along its banks, it was mesmerising to watch as the water plummeted, seemingly in slow motion, to the pools below. From certain angles, rainbows would appear in the gorge above the spray.

It was one of the most spectacular sights I had ever seen.

From Livingstone, we had travelled by bus to Lusaka to secure our visas for Mozambique and make final preparations for our entry into the country. Once we had our documents, we travelled from the city to our start point and began walking towards the border, sticking close to the Lower Zambezi National Park to our south. My companion had attempted to pass through the reserve the year before, but the eye-watering ranger fees made it impossible.

Emerging bleary-eyed from the compound in Luangwa the next morning, as the sun began to rise over the rooftops we made our way to the immigration office to get stamped out of the country. The officials seemed surprised to see us and told us that few westerners crossed into Mozambique from where we were. Writing our passport details by hand into a large scruffy notebook, they were friendly enough and dealt with us in reasonable time.

Then we wandered down the hill to the beach where the boats were gathered. The wind was causing waves on the river and it felt surprisingly cool, as I watched men unloading the boats and the women talking in agitated tones to one another. The twenty-foot-long vessels were made of fiberglass or slatted planks of wood, painted inside and out, with a small outboard engine at the stern.

Numerous boxes of fish were stacked neatly nearby, destined for the town or plates hundreds of miles away. For now, there were enough to go around, but as in other parts of Africa, little thought was given to the future, as David Lemon had lamented when he was standing in the very same spot as I, a few years earlier:

'Curious, I examined some of the parcels and was horrified to discover that most of the fish being removed from the (Cahora Bassa) lake were fingerlings or very small specimens.' (3)

Whilst in Lusaka organising our visas, I had heard that many fishermen along the Zambezi removed everything they could from the river with little thought for the future. It had saddened me that many of the fish would never reach adulthood and be able to reproduce and I wondered what future generations living by the water would eat.

We paid one of the boatmen the nominal amount of about a pound to cross into Mozambique, joining several other passengers as we climbed aboard. Pushing us away from shore into deeper water, the helmsman fired up the engine and pointed the vessel towards the east. The feeling was of real adventure and real challenge, rarely experienced when holding down a nine to five job, and I couldn't have been happier.

'No turning back now!' I muttered across to Chaz, sitting opposite.

'Yep!' He grinned broadly, nodding his head and glancing at distant hills.

The crossing took us through a stiff breeze, causing me to shiver, and we passed boats heading in the opposite direction with goods for sale: chickens in cages, fish of every description in open wooden boxes and oddly shaped exotic fruits piled high. I had learnt that there was a healthy informal trade between the two countries, with food mainly coming from Mozambique, being bartered for seemingly luxury items like radio batteries, tools and clothes from the Zambian side. Looking across the water, I saw a steep line of hills parallel with the Zambezi and hoped that our route would bypass them.

I was relieved that the expedition had got off to a good start and that we were finally on our way. We were fit, strong, lightly but reasonably well equipped and were ready to launch into the country. David Livingstone on the other hand, had an inauspicious start to his own expedition when he was bobbing around on the Indian Ocean at the mouth of the Zambezi waiting to begin. Apparently, he had been up all night with an acute attack of diarrhoea while the vessel 'rolled terribly.'

Crossing from Luangwa in Zambia into Mozambique

He noted in his journal that:

'Nothing can exceed the discomfort and pain when one is obliged to hold on with all his might to prevent being pitched off the closet'. (2)

Gently nudging the bank at Zumbo next to other craft by mid-morning, we had now entered the western end of Tete province. We gathered our gear and with the help of the boatman directing us, made our way towards the immigration office. It was our gateway into the country and we'd heard stories about travellers getting unnecessarily delayed there, so we kept our fingers crossed that we could pass through quickly.

I glanced around the town and realised why it had looked so dark the night before. There were no streetlights hanging from the overhead cables and there looked to be little life. The reason I had seen no headlights was because there were no cars on the road. We passed square plots of waste ground, covered in thorns and scrub.

David Livingstone had passed through Zumbo, then a

village, in 1856 and been impressed with the enterprise of the Jesuits who had established it in the 1500s, calling it 'the most charmingly picturesque site in the country'. As well as building a church and mission buildings, now in ruins, they had apparently made great progress in converting the locals to Christianity, something he approved highly of. He was less impressed with the evidence of the slave and ivory trade in the village though, which was used as a staging post between Central Africa and Tete, one of the main settlements and trading hubs on the Zambezi.

As someone who is deeply interested in history, I was fascinated how a European nation came to govern Mozambique, implant the Portuguese language and subjugate its people all in the name of colonial ambition. This territorial land grab preceded by a few hundred years the so called 'Scramble for Africa' and George Martelli provides an interesting historical perspective:

'The Portuguese connection with south-east Africa dated from the year 1498, when Vasco de Gama stopped at the island of Mozambique on his voyage of discovery to India. In the following century their armies, clad in mail armour and armed with matchlocks and arquebuses, ascended the Zambezi to Sena and Tete, and fought the first battles between black and white to demonstrate the superiority of gunfire over bows and arrows.' (2)

Ambling up the crumbling immigration office steps, we were met by a dour-looking older official leaning against the counter. He asked in broken English to see our papers and proceeded to take his time. Chaz and I exchanged anxious glances as we knew the man was our last barrier into the country. We had agreed not to mention that we were walking the Zambezi, in case it had to be referred to higher authority. Instead, we stated that we were just visiting the country for a few weeks to see some of the game parks and travel to the coast. Simply getting a visa to enter Mozambique had been an ordeal and had taken nearly a day of administrative woes when we passed through Lusaka a few weeks earlier, and we didn't want to increase the officialdom.

The official, on seeing an old visa for Tanzania in my passport, was adamant about checking my yellow fever inoculation certificate, even though the document had been provided during the visa application process. I started to explain this to the man, but then thought better of it and fished out the document from my pack. A little later, a younger colleague came in and we struck up a conversation to find out about the area. He told us that few white people came through Zumbo and those who did were usually overlanders looking to get off the beaten track. Eventually, after numerous questions, the review of supplementary documents, calls to the lodge we had listed as a stopping point and a few mosquito bites, the older official stamped our passports with a resounding thud and we were free to go.

Leaving the office we had a spring in our step, as even though we would have to extend our visas during the journey, probably in Tete and half way to the sea, we were now able to continue along the river. By this time, the sun finally broke through the clouds which we took as a good omen.

'He seemed quite keen to find a reason not to let us in!' I joked.

'Yeah, and you can tell that he sees so few people passing through here, that he likes to take his time to pass the day,' my companion agreed.

'Imagine if he had turned us down, after all the effort of getting here?'

We made our way back into the centre of town towards the police station, as we had been told we would need a letter to travel through the national park on the southern side of Lake Cahora Bassa. The park has a healthy population of lions and we had already arranged through one of our contacts for an armed ranger to escort us through.

The police officers, most of whom looked in their teens, were amused with our visit and I assumed, like the immigration officers, that they rarely saw western travellers in the district, particularly ones on foot. One of the officers who spoke a little English translated for the senior man sitting behind an imposing wooden desk. He asked many questions about our trip and said a letter was possible. We thanked him and his colleague proceeded to hand write something on a notepad in front of him.

Chaz and I looked sideways at each other, expecting to see even a basic computer, but went with the flow as we chatted with the other officer. He told us that crime was low in the district as the punishments were often severe, with criminals being sent to the prison in Tete. I was to find out later that the jail's inmates were rarely fed and had to rely on family members to bring them food, and frequently fell ill due to the unsanitary conditions, while violence was not uncommon.

Eventually, after more chat, the letter was completed by the senior officer and, reaching for an official looking stamp and ink pad, he said something in Portuguese to the interpreter. The man smiled and turned to us, explaining that the letter was ready, as long as we contributed to the 'whisky fund'. We had already decided that we were not going to pay bribes if we could avoid it and told the officers that we had limited money and wouldn't be able to make a contribution. The policemen smiled, shrugged their shoulders in unison and the letter was slid off the desk and disappeared.

We walked away from the police station a little dejected to plan our next course of action, and called some of our contacts in the country for further advice. There now seemed to be conflicting views about the need for a letter at all. Some said it was needed and others said it was just a scam by officials wanting to make a little extra cash. I suspected the latter.

Making our way to some shops we had seen on the way, we changed some money at a rundown shop and looked for somewhere to stay so that we could think through our options. We also wanted to get out of the sun, as the temperature was soaring and we needed to cool down. As we were chatting by a stall, the immigration official who had dealt with us earlier spotted us and held out his palms as if to say 'Why are you still here?' Smiling, we indicated that we would be moving on shortly and he slowly wandered off, glancing over his shoulder as he left.

'What's his problem?' I asked my companion, watching the figure leave.

'Oh, he probably wants us out of town, now that he's cleared us,' he answered. 'He probably thinks he now has responsibility for us and wants to see us gone from his patch.'

Zumbo had seen better days. Many of the buildings, built of brick with corrugated iron roofs, hadn't seen a lick of paint in years and looked as though they were about to collapse. The roads around the town were rutted tracks with deep holes to catch the unwary, and litter was abundant. In the centre, near to a phone shop and some bars was a market, with secondhand clothes lying forlornly in heaps, slowly being picked over by local women and their children. It wasn't the kind of place you wanted to linger. The town apparently had a population of thirty thousand, but from what I had seen while wandering along the dirty streets, there looked to be only a tenth of that in residence.

During the civil war, the town's strategic location made it a vital access point for ammunition and supplies and consequently it bore the brunt of some of the fighting. Zumbo was abandoned for a time during the conflict and much of the promised reconstruction was never completed. Landmines were laid on the outskirts of the town, making it impossible for locals to harvest crops and go about their normal lives, but the devices continued to cause many deaths and injuries long after the fighting was over.

At a place with a neat thatched roof and freshly painted yellow walls, a Zimbabwean woman called Grace rented us a room with a normal bed against the wall and a mattress on the floor. Pleased to be out of the sun and making ourselves comfortable with some cold Cokes, we pulled out maps and satnav devices and made some more calls to our local contacts to work out a plan for the way ahead. Needing a few supplies, I strolled out of the compound a little later and bought some biscuits and fruit. The pile of secondhand clothes was still being picked over and I wondered what the locals had to look forward to in their lives, in a town where little happened and where the government obviously showed scant interest. I saw little reason for people wanting to come here, apart from travellers like us just passing through.

Towards evening, we pulled together the three possible options for our journey. First, to walk on the south side of Cahora Bassa Lake and through the national park with a guide, but unarmed (the option of having an armed guide through the park had disappeared during the day). Second, to walk on the south side of the lake but along the tarmac roads well below it and outside the national park. The third option was to walk along the north shore, something we had previously discounted, as our contacts had said that it was a wild place with scores of dangerous animals, venomous snakes, hilly terrain and overgrown vegetation.

We discussed each option at length over a dinner of fish covered in tomatoes and afterwards, as the sun was going down, stepped out to find a bar to chew it over some more. As we sipped cold drinks under an open-sided hut and reflected on the day, young children dressed in ragged clothes played football on a dusty pitch behind us, their cries of joy and excitement carrying in the still air.

As we mulled over the route some more, I reflected on what David Lemon had decided to do long before arriving in country:

'I had decided that although the southern shoreline of Cahora Bassa contained a lot less in the way of wildlife, it offered considerably easier walking as most of it was flat. The northern bank appeared very rocky and mountainous, so the decision was easily made.' (3)

To me the choice was clear, to walk along the north shore. It would be a real adventure and take us away from the difficulties of the national park on the south side. It was also where David Livingstone had trekked a hundred and fifty years previously on his own Zambezi expedition. Chaz was less enthusiastic, preferring the southern shore but conceding that a trek along partially tarmacked roads there was less appealing. We both agreed that taking an unarmed guide through the park was risky, because even though he would know the routes, the threat of lions was a real one.

Eventually, we both agreed that the northern route was the one to take and even though it was wild country, we felt that it would give us the adventure we were seeking.

Chapter Two - Lake Cahora Bassa

After a breakfast of tea and biscuits and saying goodbye to Grace, we headed out of Zumbo. Mozambique seems to be a magnet for displaced people from the region and I came across numerous workers from neighbouring countries including Zambia, Malawi, South Africa and Zimbabwe during the journey.

We trekked along an uneven track, with stunted scrub on either side, catching occasional glimpses of the Zambezi and passing through a few small settlements along the way. Dubbed 'God's Highway' by David Livingstone, he viewed the river as an opportunity to bring both Christianity and civilisation to the unreached peoples of Central Africa. As we walked, I reminded Chaz about the landmine threat and we stuck to the track like glue, not even leaving it if we needed to pee.

It was a Sunday and walking past one of the churches, we heard gospel singing ringing out which was quite beautiful. Men and women's voices moving up and down the scales came together in perfect harmony as they celebrated their God. I was tempted to go inside for a better look, but thought better of it bearing in mind my attire and unkempt appearance. The locals we saw on the road, with skin the colour of teak and dressed in tatty clothes with some burdened with heavy bags, were friendly enough, but with our packs, trekking gear and sunglasses, we felt a little out of place and they studied us suspiciously, probably not having seen many white people in the area before.

At one point, near to what looked like a school, a huge mechanical drill sitting on top of a truck was scouring out red earth all over the track we were on and making a racket. There are few water systems in northern Mozambique and people have to drill for a well on their land or fetch it from the river or a communal pump. The workmen we spoke to were trying to tap into the water table so that a pump could be installed for the school and the children didn't have to risk a visit to the river. Crocodiles live along most of the Zambezi's length and locals are often taken when they linger close to the water.

Arriving at the lodge after a few hours of steady walking, we were greeted with a wonderful cup of fresh coffee and its manger, Calvin, had agreed to put us up. The waiters had been expecting us and a lunch of freshly made, piping hot lasagne followed shortly afterwards as Chaz and I grinned at our good fortune. Calvin and his family were out, so we took the opportunity to have a look around and play with their young dog who had been left to stand guard.

Chawalo Lodge sits in a beautiful setting overlooking one of the many waterways at the western end of the Cahora Bassa lake. The main building was an open air, solid stone structure with a neatly trimmed thatched roof and a 180-degree view of the water. It was surrounded by manicured green grass and had chalets dotted around the grounds, one of which was lent to us. Neat, stone walkways connected all the buildings and it was clear to see that the site had been well planned. The chalet was sumptuous, with comfortable beds protected with mosquito nets, hot running water, fresh white towels and a porch for sitting and discussing our plans, overlooking a dried-up pond. Small lizards darted around the stonework when they saw us and songbirds flitted from branch to branch on the nearby trees. It was great to have some luxury for a change and we felt as if we really had landed on our feet.

Later, we met up with Calvin and his family, who were interested in our endeavour and offered to put their network at our disposal in case we needed help. Calvin was from Zimbabwe, had run the lodge for several years and was a classic African outdoorsman, with rugged suntanned features and a happy-go-lucky attitude. He was keen to take us out in his boat, a small white fibreglass affair with large outboard motor, to look for elephants. Weaving around the many islands, we spotted numerous crocodiles, some of them huge, basking on the banks until they slid into the water on our approach. A few pods of hippos eyed us suspiciously and trumpeted in annoyance at being disturbed before slipping gracefully below the surface. Sadly, the elephants weren't visible but Calvin assured us they were there, as evidenced by footprints in the mud.

'They feel safe on the islands, as few people ever come,' he told us. 'Thankfully, the villagers don't kill them as happens in other parts of Africa, as they believe they are their ancestors. Occasionally the herd will raid the crops near a village, but get chased off and head into thick bush.'

'What about the hippos?'

'Ah, that's a different story' Calvin replied. 'They won't allow themselves to be intimidated when tucking into the village vegetable patch and have been known to charge and kill locals who try to scare them off.'

At over two hundred and eighty kilometres long and over thirty kilometres at its widest point, Lake Cahora Bassa was a major feature on our journey. With the limited mapping that was available, I had estimated that it could take up to two weeks to traverse. The lake was created when the dam of the same name was built near the Cahora Bassa rapids, near to the town of Songo at its eastern end. The dam, finished in 1974 and one of the largest in Africa, produces hydro-electric power, most of which is sold to its southern neighbours.

The lake's main industry is fishing for kapenta, small inch-sized fish that are fried and eaten with nshima, a local staple made of maize flour. Tiger fish are also found in the lake and dedicated fishermen from around the world travel on tours to the water to battle with the ferocious and infamous giant. Zambezi sharks, otherwise known as bull sharks and able to live in fresh water, are also known to inhabit the lake, having been cut off from the sea when the dam was built. Our host explained that on the north shore, there were also crocodile farms which bred the reptiles and used the skins to make luxury goods like handbags and shoes.

As we returned to the lodge, Calvin told us about the

poaching of animals in the area by the locals and how a market had developed in selling meat, other body parts and claws from the big cats to Chinese workers in the country. China had been given large forestry concessions in Mozambique recently and huge trucks carrying the logs made frequent trips to the ports. Many a time over the coming weeks I would be covered in dust from these passing trucks, as they made their way to the coast. It was the Chinese forestry workers who also bought the exotic animal parts and took them home when on leave to earn extra cash.

Later, Chaz and I met up with Calvin and his kids in the bar and enjoyed cold beer and biltong, whilst watching a South African rugby game. The bar was up in the eaves of the main building and had a superb view over the grounds leading down to the water. We fed well that night on a dinner of succulent beef, fresh vegetables and piping hot fried potatoes, washed down with a glass of finest claret. We both knew that we would be living rough for most of the journey and resorting to pasta mixed with dried soup for our evening meals, so didn't mind accepting such generosity when it was offered.

Chatting over dinner, it was clear that Calvin had set up an interesting life with his family in Mozambique. He was miles away from his home country and despite the hardships and frustrations of living there, including the Mozambican bureaucracy, harsh terrain and dangerous animals on his doorstep, he had made a life for himself that many would envy.

Wandering back to the chalet, my friend and I congratulated each other on how well the start of the expedition had gone. A few days earlier we had been across the border in Luangwa not knowing what to expect, but now we were on our way and our good fortune was holding. As we neared the chalet, a mosquito bit me behind the ear, followed by another one biting me on the hand – it was a price worth paying to be in a such a beautiful spot so close to the water, but I was keen to slide under my net. On his travels along the Zambezi, David Livingstone summed up the threat very well:

'The miserable and sleepless night that only one mosquito inside the curtain can cause, is so well known… one soon learns, from experience, that to beat out the curtains thoroughly before entering them, so that not one of these pests can possibly be harboured within, is the only safeguard against such severe trials to one's tranquillity and temper'. (1)

The following day, after a tasty breakfast of bacon, beans, scrambled eggs and coffee, we said goodbye to our wonderful hosts and hoisted on our packs. Setting off from the lodge, we walked through the undergrowth close to the water, a line of rolling hills off to our left. Calvin had warned us about snakes in the area and had recounted a tale of finding two black mambas in the grounds of the lodge a year earlier.

I knew the black mamba was definitely one to avoid. It's a highly venomous snake, endemic to parts of sub-Saharan Africa, often growing to over three metres in length. Unlike other snakes in the region, it has a reputation for standing its ground rather than slithering away. Although we had first aid kits and knowledge of how to treat basic injuries, we didn't have anti-venom, due to the variety of snakes in the country, nor a means of refrigeration and for most of the trip would be many miles from any hospital or clinic. Despite the threat, we had to push on and make ground through the high grass, often up to our chests, hoping not to come across one. I coined the phrase 'snakey snakey grass' and it was a phrase we returned to quite often. Snakes are not able to hear but they do feel vibrations and when we struggled to see our feet through the vegetation, we would bang the ground with our shoes to let them know we were coming through. Thankfully, we didn't see any snakes that morning, but we knew that they would always be close by.

Another threat so close to the water were hippos that feasted on the lush year-round vegetation. We saw their tracks everywhere and their mud slides back into the water, and every so often we would stop to listen out for them. Over five hundred people are killed by hippos every year in Africa and we both understood the danger they posed. We found that their deep tracks in the mud, hardened by the sun, made walking quite difficult in places and turning an ankle was a constant worry.

The wind had been quite strong all morning, keeping us cool and the flies and mosquitoes away, but we knew they would return when the wind abated; being next to the water was always going to bring with it the dreaded mosquito. Thankfully, we had good anti-malarial tablets, sprays and secure bug nets within our tents. Malaria is the biggest killer in Mozambique, with nearly a thousand deaths every year from over four million cases reported. We knew that the provinces we would be travelling through, namely Tete, Sofala, Manica and Zambezia were particularly susceptible to the disease and we would have to be on our guard all the time. The government and international charities gave out millions of impregnated mosquito nets every year, but it seemed to have little effect. In some communities by the water, particularly closer to the ocean, I would see the blue nets being used to catch small fish, as the mesh was the perfect size for trapping them.

A little later, we stumbled across some women, resplendent in their flowing and colourful clothes, some with babies wrapped in shawls on their backs, doing their washing down by the lake. Clothes that had been washed and laid on bushes nearby, were fluttering gently in the breeze. As they caught sight of us coming out of the bush, they stopped what they were doing and gazed at us in surprise. One of the small children ran up the bank into the bush, presumably in fear, shouting 'Mzungu! Mzungu!' the name given for a white man in many parts of Africa. We might have been the first white people he had ever seen. Offering a greeting to our audience, we smiled and waved at the women and after a brief pause, when they realised we weren't a threat, they went back to their laundry duties, although kept a close eye on us as we strolled past.

The ground near the water became marshy and overgrown, difficult to get through, and several times the water came up to my shins. We therefore decided to cut inland to try to find a track parallel with the lake and, after a few wrong turns, found what we were looking for. The path twisted and turned through the dense bush and every so often hit a dry river bed of deep sand and stones.

As we approached one of these river beds further inland, we saw a small Isuzu truck stuck fast in the sand with its well-dressed passengers looking at it, hands on hips and wondering what to do. Their smart, clean attire suggested that they might be charity workers and they seemed reluctant to dirty their clothes and push the vehicle out. As Chaz and I were already sweaty and grubby from traipsing through bush and wanted to do the right thing, we took off our packs and stepped forward to help.

Scooping out the sand around the wheels, we grabbed a few nearby logs and forced them under the tyres to allow some better purchase. The driver turned the wheels slowly but there was no grip between rubber and wood and the truck sank lower into the sand. Bigger and bigger logs were required to prevent the wheels from spinning and eventually, after I had taken over the driving duties, we managed to get the vehicle out and on to firmer ground. Our new friends were delighted with our efforts and there were handshakes all round. Their pristine clothes were still intact, whereas my companion and I were even filthier than before and covered in sweat, but we were happy that we had helped out fellow travellers in need.

'Hopefully, that'll bring us some good karma,' noted my companion, as we gathered up our things.

'Yep,' I agreed. 'Who knows when we'll need help?'

'Just when you think all is well on these kind of trips, Murphy's law has a habit of kicking you where it hurts!' he grinned as we waved goodbye and continued east.

We trudged on, trying to maintain a consistent bearing but

it was difficult as the track would split and it was often hard deciding which route to take. By now, we were out of sight of the lake and no longer able to use it as a reference point. Eventually, we entered a small village seeking directions to Chantanda, our planned stopping point for the day. Music blared out from speakers on a table and about twenty men in small groups were slumped against the huts and buildings in various states of drunkenness. Walking over to some of the more sober looking locals to ask for directions, we were met with wafts of their hands to somewhere in the distance, over our shoulders. Forfeiting the opportunity for a fizzy drink, we moved off into the shade to review our satnav and gather our bearings, then decided it looked a dodgy place and got moving again.

We were crossing a small football pitch when two of the men, stinking of beer, latched on to us. I explained as best as I could that we didn't need any help, but they just grunted something in Portuguese and pointed along the track. Chaz then set off again at a fast pace and I shouted after him to slow down as I thought the men, although annoying, were harmless. Ignoring my pleas without looking around, he increased his stride, disappearing around a corner followed by one of the men. This annoyed me, as I knew we had to stick together. I began to try to communicate with the remaining man who smiled, giving me a bleary look through his bloodshot eyes. They were just interested to see where we were going and probably hoping to earn some loose change for their next fix of beer.

'Go home!' I instructed the man, pointing back to the village, but my new companion just lolled his head and drew his hand slowly across his face.

Continuing, I found my trekking companion about a kilometre along the track, taking shade under a tree. I told him the men were harmless and that we wouldn't be able to outrun them anyway, particularly as we had packs on and they would know the area like the back of their hands. It was crazy to go so fast in the heat when we didn't have to.

Reluctantly, he nodded in agreement and after a quick drink of water, we carried on with our interlopers, this time at a slower, steadier pace.

After an hour of following the track, which twisted and turned through the scrub, we reached the small settlement of Chantanda, hidden behind a wall of trees and vegetation, and asked around if anyone spoke English. We were directed to a hut and were introduced to Chris, a slim man dressed in dark trousers and clean white shirt. Through dazzling white teeth, he explained to us that he was a teacher and happy to help and knew somewhere where we could stay. As we were chatting, one of the men who had followed us and was now sitting on a stool he had found shouted out to him. There followed an animated conversation as my companion and I glanced uneasily at each other.

'He is asking if you are going to pay them now,' Chris finally informed us.

'For what?' I replied, looking over at the two men.

'He says they guided you here and you agreed to pay them,' said our helper, breathing out hard.

'No, that's not true. They tagged on to us at the last village, even though we didn't want their help. I told them to go home, but they kept following.'

Chris explained this to the men, who sighed and shook their heads in disappointment, sending a few choice words in Portuguese our way. Picking themselves up, they trundled back along the path into the bush, disappearing in seconds. The teacher turned and led us along a winding path through the scrub to a ranger camp by the lake. It was an attractive spot with canvas tents set up in a clearing and had an elevated position over a lagoon surrounded by tall grasses a hundred metres away. In the distance I could just make out some hippos relaxing in the river, the occasional grunt carrying in the breeze. We asked our host if we could stay there and he said that the rangers would be happy to agree and so we found a flat area near some trees, erected our tents and made some tea.

Once established, I walked down to the water for a much-needed wash, keeping a lookout for crocodiles. I knew they were close by because I could see their claw marks in a mud bank near to where I stood. I witnessed in Kenya a few years earlier the frightening speed the animals can launch out of the water. There were some small boats nearby and a piece of soap in the grass gave it away as a communal washing point.

Later, the rangers in olive-green uniforms returned to camp and their broad smiles seemed to indicate that they were happy to see us. We explained what we were doing there and on their walkie-talkies they called Andreas, the Spanish owner of both the camp and a lodge further along the lake. Giving his blessing for our stay at the ranger camp, he also invited us to his lodge the following day. We were delighted that we were getting this much support so early in the trip. It seemed we were uncovering a network of lodges dotted along the shore.

To celebrate, when Chris returned to the camp later, we asked if he could acquire us some chicken and nshima from the village for supper. I had eaten nshima in Zambia in the weeks previously and found the texture and taste very uninspiring, but it was at least filling and usually hot, so had grown accustomed to it. Agreeing a price for the food, we settled down on some benches under a thatch roof to chat about the day, review our maps and watch the sun setting over the water. We were both excited to be camping at such a scenic spot, as noisy birds close by disturbed our chatter and began to roost.

When the food arrived, we were given plastic plates onto which nshima and a few pieces of chicken in gravy were placed. Another older man had come with Chris to carry the food. The meat didn't look fully cooked in my torchlight and the nshima was glutinous and bland. Knowing we had a long trek the following day, I ate what I could and passed my plate over to our host, who finished it off rapidly. We thanked the men for their efforts, and they walked off into the darkness and back to their homes.

Once the mosquitoes had found us, we both retired to our tents to get away from the onslaught and catch some rest. I only had a narrow, albeit light tent and had to take great care not to rest my arms against the internal net, otherwise the pests would bite right through it. On the opposite side of the lake to where we were staying, David Lemon recalled his own experiences:

'The further down the lake I trudged, the worse the mosquitos became. When I packed up camp in the mornings, they would fly around me in a dense cloud and throughout the day I would be subject to their depredations.' (3)

The night started off warm enough and initially I lay on my sleeping mat in just shorts and shirt, but in the early hours the temperature plummeted and I had to climb into my sleeping bag liner and put on my trousers and thin fleece to get warm. We hadn't brought sleeping bags, as we wanted to travel as light as possible, but I regretted that decision for most of the journey, as on some nights it was bitterly cold.

Emerging from our tents the next morning, it was clear that Chaz hadn't slept well either, as he stretched his limbs, wiped sleep from his eyes and began to make a fire. After a quick breakfast, we packed up, refilled our water bottles from the lake and set off on a forty-kilometre hike to the Kwanda camp. It was still cool and we were both warming up after the cold night, but it was good to be moving again and stretching the muscles.

The track we were on weaved through the bush, crossing over riverbed after riverbed. Coming up a rise after a few hours, we spotted a small clinic complex, a few simple brick-built structures clustered together and headed for it. Expectant mothers sat in the shade, a look of contentment on their faces, and we were shown to a water pump where we filled up our bottles. We learnt later that the facility was built by the owner of the lodge we were heading for, as a goodwill gesture and a sign of investing in the community. As we were learning, the infrastructure in the country was quite poor and development money is concentrated in the south, so the northern provinces have to make do or do without altogether. Some of the expat-owned lodges try to help out the communities by building clinics, schools and water boreholes.

We were hoping for a shop to buy fizzy drinks, to take away the earthy taste of the Zambezi water in our bottles, but there was none, so we settled for some cold fritters instead. They were being sold by a young boy no older than ten and he took our money gratefully. Devouring them in the shade, we were surrounded by inquisitive children, smiling and laughing at our antics. As I was eating, I glanced up casually and spotted a large, black palm-sized spider hanging from the porch.

A smart looking man walked over to us, explained that he was the headmaster of the local school and asked us, in an official tone, who we were and what we were doing. Although I understood Mozambique's recent history, I always found it slightly irritating to be asked for documents and to explain myself. We disclosed that we were walking the Zambezi through the country and he told us that it couldn't be done, although didn't provide any evidence for his assertion. He asked for our documents once more, hands on hips and glaring as we shrugged our shoulders. Once the man realised that we weren't going to comply, his manner relented a little and he said that he would direct us and lead us through the village and onto the right path. In the centre, I noticed that tracks led everywhere and realised that his help was invaluable.

On the outskirts of the village, after we had got to know the headmaster a little better and his temperament had thawed further, we rewarded our new friend with a 'Crazy Cola' a derivative of the famous drink and some biscuits from a small shop. Waving us off, the man trudged back the way we had come.

We then walked for hours through the hot, dry bush, passing spindly trees which had managed to retain some green foliage. On our left and right were sand coloured grasses, burnt to a crisp by the sun and brittle to the touch. The going at this point was fairly even, with an occasional hillock to climb and we passed through few settlements. The locals that we did see would eye us suspiciously when we appeared, until their uncertainty evaporated with our smiles and waves and they would then reciprocate, flashing their bright, white teeth at us. Occasionally, we would take water if there was a pump in the village, but often we just pressed on.

Chaz and I could go for hours without talking, as we took in the setting, shouldered our burdens and enjoyed the challenge we had undertaken. Taciturn in nature, he often kept his thoughts to himself, but enjoyed a joke and a chat when there was a break in the trekking, or when we were warming ourselves by the fire after a hard day in the bush.

At one point the path swung back towards the lake and we took the opportunity to walk next to the water for a while. We saw a few large crocodiles basking in the sun, but they slid quickly into the water, spooked by our presence. Taking water from the lake, we each made some soup in the shade of some overhanging branches and using our packs as seats took the weight off our feet.

'This is the life, mate!' I grinned, and took a sip of the soup.

'Agreed! A perfect rest stop, apart from the crocodiles.'

I guessed that the land we were sitting on wasn't owned by anyone as it was so remote, but it did look an ideal spot for fishing. Whilst in Lusaka, I had bought some fish hooks and line, to allow us to catch our dinner when the opportunity arose. There's nothing quite like the fresh taste of fish cooked over an open fire, something I had experienced many times in the wild before, and I was determined to try when I got a chance.

Later, as we trekked along the shoreline and I was scanning the ground for anything interesting, I spotted something strange sticking out of the sand. Moving closer, I recognised the rusting tailfin of a mortar. I called Chaz over for a look and told him what it was. It seemed a strange spot, in the middle of nowhere, to be aiming mortars, but I knew that fighting in the civil war had taken place all over the country, including around the lake, and thought that there might have been a skirmish close to where we now stood.

The Mozambique Civil War lasted from 1977 to 1992 and over a million people died, with several million displaced. Mozambique was declared free of mines in 2015, only two years before our trek, but it was always at the back of our minds when moving through the bush. Throughout the trip, I spotted empty bullet cases by the side of the road or track, particularly near built-up areas and bridges.

Back inland, as we rounded a corner we saw a vehicle racing towards us, a dust cloud swirling behind it. Two white men were sitting in front and some locals were in the back dressed in ranger gear. Slowing down, it stopped next to us and the man held up his hand in greeting. It was Andreas, the owner of the lodge, who was heading to Zumbo to meet with officials and shop for supplies. He confirmed his offer for us to stay at the lodge and gave brief directions, before racing off again in a cloud of dirt. We now had something definite to aim for. Walking around the Lower Zambezi National Park, on our way to Luangwa and the start of our expedition, we had slept in schools, churches and camped in the bush and had taken up offers of hospitality whenever they arose.

Continuing, we walked ever eastwards, hardly seeing a soul for the next few hours. The track went up and down, left and right, through streambeds and on and on. The heat was oppressive and we had to keep drinking water to stay hydrated, although catching a glimpse of the lake in the distance calmed our fears of running out of fluid.

At one point, we passed through a large banana plantation, the green fruit ripening in the sunshine. It was the first sign we had seen of organised farming, as normally villagers would just grow a few crops near their huts, and we wondered if it was a collective of some kind. We passed a few workers relaxing in the shade and eating bananas. They studied us intently as we strolled past. A few kilometres further on, we crossed over a sandy, dry river bed where the sun's rays bounced off the pale surface and dazzled our eyes.

Later, in the heat of the day, we finally ran out of water, but continued on in the hope of finding some in due course. Although only a few kilometres from the lake, we knew it would take hours to get there, take us off course and involve an excursion through thorny scrub and marsh. As our throats became parched and the sweat on our faces turned to salt, we stumbled over a rise on the track and spotted a stream under a thick canopy of vegetation a short distance away and raced thankfully towards it. The depth of the water was only a few inches, but it was cool and refreshing and we sat down on some rocks, drank our fill and washed the sweat and grime off our faces. It felt so good to move water around my mouth, which a few minutes earlier had been dry as a bone. It was a salient lesson for both of us, even though we were experienced outdoors people. We had begun the day with full bottles, filled up at every opportunity and still it wasn't enough.

'Close one that, mate!' I smiled at my companion.

'Yeah, too close,' he replied, taking another swig.

'Reckon I'm going to carry more. This place is like a furnace.'

'Can't be that far away now?' he asked, checking his satnav and glancing along the track.

We had to be close. We'd been walking for nine hours now. We had checked our devices at most stops and knew how far we had come, but as the lodge wasn't marked, it was difficult to work out how far we still had to go. The track we were on was edging towards the lake, but as yet not touching it.

Pulling on our packs, we trundled on in silence without seeing a soul. Eventually, turning a corner a little later, we saw a battered sign nailed to a tree. The writing was old and worn, but it definitely said 'Kwanda!' There was no need for a fancy sign, as this was no five-star hotel with hundreds of guests; this was an exclusive retreat for a select few who guarded their privacy.

Staggering slowly towards the lodge, we passed a few outlying huts that looked like workers' quarters and heard some goats bleating, oblivious to their fate. We walked towards the main buildings and were greeted by a smart looking local, who guided us to some lounge chairs overlooking the water. He disappeared and returned shortly afterwards with a tray of cold drinks and water, along with a plate of bananas, probably from the plantation we had passed through. It was so good to take the weight off our feet after a long day and relax on soft comfortable chairs in the shade! The lodge was similar in design to the one we had stayed in a few days earlier, stone construction with open air communal rooms and a neatly thatched roof.

As we were chatting, a lean white man dressed in bush gear walked over to us and introduced himself. Hayden was from South Africa, he explained, and was the professional hunter for the lodge. I had suspected that there would be hunting in Mozambique but now it was confirmed. I'm not a fan of the sport, preferring to see animals living and roaming free, but had to accept that it went on and as the lodge was helping us out, knew I would have to bite my tongue on my views. The man told us that all the rooms were taken, but that we could use his room for showers and pitch our tents by the water.

Once clean and refreshed, I tried to repair my inflatable sleeping mat that had been pierced by thorns over the previous days. Chaz gave me a few patches and glue to keep them in place, but the intervention didn't work and I was unable to inflate it for the rest of the journey and had to be satisfied just with the minimal foam inside. For weeks to come, I would wake up in the tent stiff and sore from lying on the cold, hard ground, cursing the thorns and my choice of mat.

Putting the frustration to one side, we walked down to the

lake to see if we could spot crocodiles, but there were none to be seen, probably hiding in the cooling waters. The lodge was set in beautiful surroundings on sloping ground and nestled in between a wide variety of trees. Acacias, mahogany and a large baobab tree behind the main building provided a blanket of shade from the blistering sun. A lawn of coarse grass led down to a sandy bay on the lake. A few chalets were connected by a stony path, each with magnificent views over the nearby islands and water.

My trekking gear was filthy from the long day through the bush and after giving it a good wash, I joined the others in the bar to await the arrival of Andreas. Over cold beers, Hayden told us about the hunting in the area and the clients of the lodge.

'What are the main predators on this side of the lake?' I asked.

'We have leopards here, which like to live around the kopjes in the hills. It's perfect for them; plenty of cover, rocky terrain and lots of game,' he answered.

'Do you think we'll see any?' I enquired.

'Unlikely. They're pretty secretive animals and operate mainly at night, so you're unlikely to spot them. I know there's quite a population further down the lake, still on this side, so if you end up there you might come across them.'

'And do you get many?'

'A few a year. That's all we're allowed to take and besides, we want an active population and are not here to kill them all off.'

'What about lions?'

'Nah, I don't think they're here anymore. I've been coming to this place for a few years now and have heard stories of sightings from some of the villages out in the wilderness, but I've not seen any evidence. They're on the southern side of Cahora Bassa for sure, where there are good numbers.'

'So, who comes here to hunt then?' asked Chaz, shifting in his chair.

I knew that he also didn't approve of hunting, but we were guests.

'Mainly rich Americans, but sometimes Russians. They fly in to Lusaka, we meet them and bring them over the border to here. They usually stay for a week and we take them on several hunts, starting with the herbivores, deer, waterbuck, nyala, that kind of thing. Sometimes we'll take a crocodile if we go out in the boats. If we have licences left for leopard, then they'll probably take one towards the end of the week.'

'That must cost a pretty penny?' I asked.

'Yeah. Big bucks,' answered the hunter, nodding his head slowly. 'This isn't a sport for those on welfare.'

Changing the subject, I asked about snakes.

'This place is full of mambas, cobras and puff adders,' smiled the South African. 'I see them often when I'm out. The black mambas can get huge out here, well over ten foot!'

'Need to steer clear of them,' I said.

'You guys also need to watch out for the scorpions in this region. Some of them are deadly and all will give a nasty sting. Watch out for the ones with small pincers and a fat tail; they're the killers. We get them in our rooms all the time. They're inquisitive buggers, always crawling about and looking for something to eat. They particularly like the showers, where it's warm and damp, so tread carefully!'

As we were talking, I glanced down at my index fingers which were strangely itchy. I noticed that there was a rash running down the outside of both digits from the knuckle to beyond the joint. They were tender to the touch and fluid seemed to be building up underneath the skin. I had been taking doxycycline tablets for the prevention of malaria for several weeks and put the rash down to a reaction from the sun, which had seemed fiercer in preceding days.

The light slowly disappeared and eventually we saw the torches of the owner's boat dance on the water as it turned into the bay. Andreas was a tall, big chested Spaniard with silvery hair and beard, weather beaten looks and smiling face. Greeting us warmly, he explained that his late arrival was due to tracking a problem hippo that was causing havoc to the crops of a local village. He told us that the animal had to be taken out, for as well as the damage to crops, it had also attacked people in recent days. It was a sobering thought as we sat down for dinner, enjoying the hospitality on offer.

After the meal and a glass of fine red wine, we chatted with our fellow diners for a while before taking our leave and making our way back to our tents. It was a chilly evening, as the wind blew in across the water but within minutes I was in a deep sleep, exhausted from the exertions and tensions of the day.

Chapter Three - Snake Central

Leaving Kwanga Lodge after breakfast, with all its luxury, tranquillity and security, felt like stepping back into the unknown. We had been told there were other lodges on the shores of the lake, but that they were few and far between. We were heading back into the bush, where our knowledge of the terrain, despite discussions at the lodge, was sketchy at best.

Andreas had lent us two of his rangers to guide us along the lake and through the scrub and Chaz and I had to increase our usual pace to keep up with our unencumbered friends.

After an hour of fast trekking, past kopjes and through light woodland, the path curled back towards the lake and the guides pointed the way to go, shook our hands and turned back. We found ourselves at a beautiful bay, the waves gently lapping against the sand and shingle shore. In the distance, a kilometre away, we could see one of the many low-lying islands, covered in tall green and yellowing grasses. On previous occasions when we had been close to the water, we had seen occasional fishermen in dugout canoes casting their flimsy nets, but now there wasn't another person to be seen. We were once again back in the wild and taking a moment to enjoy the setting, we lowered our bottles into the lake for some water before setting off along the beach.

Keeping well back from the water's edge, we made steady progress through the sand and shale. Glancing over my shoulder, I spotted a large crocodile swimming parallel to the shore, its sleek design barely visible above the water.

'Do you think it's tracking us?' asked Chaz, eying the creature.

'Probably,' I said. 'They have to take their opportunities out here. The length of the open shoreline means they have to patrol along the banks, as waiting in ambush at one spot is unlikely to work. We're fine where we are though.'

'Yeah, you can be the first line of defence then,' my friend laughed, stepping further inshore and nodding towards more crocodiles in the distance.

The Nile crocodile grows up to five metres in length and is an apex predator, taking a variety of animals for food. The huge beasts were basking on the soft mud, mouths agape to regulate their temperature. As we neared one, it sensed us crunching over the stones and within seconds had slipped underwater with barely a ripple. Further on, we came across more crocodiles sunning themselves in some reeds, and they charged into the water on seeing us. Others crashed through the shallows in spectacular fashion, water exploding everywhere, unable to get away from us fast enough. The animals obviously had a fear of humans in these parts, probably due to hunting, and during the journey I heard many stories of people being attacked by them.

Close to the water we came across a number of fishing camps, some of which had been abandoned. They were simple structures with a wooden frame, dried reeds for a roof, often open around the sides. Old fishing nets, makeshift floats and line lay discarded inside and simple cots, raised above the ground for sleeping, had collapsed on the floor. We wondered why they had been left. I was always cautious when looking around as they were a perfect habitat for scorpions and snakes, being shady with plenty of places to hide.

We trekked along the shoreline of the Cahora Bassa for several hours and hoped that we could stay by the water, but then began to hit lagoons stretching northwards. Initially, they were a few hundred metres long and fairly easy to circumvent, but as we progressed, they became longer and took more time to get around. The satnav was not accurate enough to show these features, so we had to navigate by sight and compass. Most of the lagoons had resident crocodiles and after a quick discussion, we decided to cut inland to find a track that would allow better progress.

Spotting an overgrown path leaving the lake, we took it and passed through a small settlement with children playing in the dirt and watchful mothers eying us curiously. Offering greetings in our few words of Portuguese, we checked our compasses and took the path out of the place, which was in the general direction we wanted.

In the afternoon, we arrived at a settlement consisting of a few huts and, needing to take a break, asked if they had a 'banca' or shop. A boy guided us to a rickety structure made of mud and wood, a simple padlock hanging on the door. We asked if it could be opened and he called to a young woman who came over brandishing a key. Once the door creaked open, we could see that there were soft drinks, biscuits, rice, soap and a few other items stacked neatly on the shelves; standard fare for a local banca. We asked how much the drinks would cost, but the woman just placed her hands on her hips and looked at us blankly. Pressing the point, we asked again how much she wanted, but she just shook her head slowly and stared back.

'This must be the only shop in Mozambique that doesn't want to sell anything,' my companion said irritably, spotting some tomatoes in the gloomy corner.

'Yeah. Maybe the items can only be sold to villagers? Perhaps it's more of a store for locals than a shop?' I offered.

'Maybe. I fancy those tomatoes though if they'll give them up.'

Chaz tried one more time by brandishing some meticais, the local currency, and pointing at the vegetables, but the woman just looked at him again, shaking her head. It was possible that it was just a store but it seemed strange she wouldn't sell us anything.

We trudged out of the place disconsolately, hoping to find somewhere else to buy drinks, and carried on under the burning sun. By now it was in the mid-thirties centigrade and the dry heat sapped our strength and evaporated our sweat before we noticed it. On one rest stop in the shade, I was alarmed to see that the tops of my hands were turning bright red and hurriedly applied some sun cream to try to protect them.

The path led us through a number of abandoned overgrown villages, with huts leaning over at strange angles and holes in the thatch. I wondered if they had been deserted due to the civil war, or if the villagers had just moved on to a better spot.

As I was leading our way through the bush, I turned a corner and saw a large hole to the side of the path, slightly hidden by vegetation. Walking up to it slowly, I saw a flash of scales and disturbed water, as whatever it was retreated back into its hole. Grooves in the mud, about six inches across, led from its lair into the bush and I assumed that I had met my first python in Mozambique. I would see similar burrows, often near under-used paths, on a few other occasions. Although not venomous, the python can deliver a nasty bite leading to infection, so they are best avoided. They can grow over five metres in length and lie in ambush waiting for small deer and other herbivores to pass by. Once they have struck their prey with backward facing teeth, they wrap their coils around it causing suffocation, before consuming it head first. Surprising for such a large reptile, they can survive without eating for months at a time, but when they do eat, the prey is often large, taking days to digest.

The dusty trails near Lake Cahora Bassa

As the day drew on, we started to look for somewhere to camp and came across a small hamlet in a peaceful setting close to the water, the calm destroyed by a few yapping dogs that nipped at our feet. We greeted the older man coming out of a well-built hut, who pushed the dogs away and began to speak to us in English. He was from Zimbabwe, but had left in the 1980s when the country took a turn for the worse and had settled here with his younger wife and children. There were a few chickens wandering around the yard and some vegetable patches close to the huts and it was good to see that he was making the best of his surroundings.

'Would you go back to Zimbabwe?' I asked the man.

'Nothing for me there now,' he replied bitterly, throwing a stick at one of the dogs that had crept closer. 'Besides, if I did go back, Mugabe's thugs would arrest me and throw me in jail.'

'But he isn't going to last forever and the army won't allow his wife to take over, so maybe there's a new dawn coming to the country,' I said optimistically.

'No, I'll live out my days here in peace,' he said looking around.

It certainly was a pleasant spot, although to live in such remoteness wasn't for everyone. It looked like he had enough food, with his chickens and crops and he probably bartered for fish, but I felt a little sad for the man forced to live in such isolation. We asked him where we could camp and he pointed to a small ridge a few kilometres away in the distance, so we headed for it, crossing over undulating and cracked earth.

Arriving at the place, we found a couple of abandoned shacks with discarded fishing detritus that overlooked a marshy creek. It was a wonderful location, with an expansive view of the lake in the distance, birds swooping down to the water and a slight breeze to cool us after a heavy day. Evergreen bushes, spindly trees and thorny scrub dotted the view and there wasn't a cloud to be seen.

As I was erecting my tent, Chaz called me over urgently,

telling me there was a snake in the hut he was in! I stepped cautiously over, asking what kind it was and he informed me that it was small, only about twelve inches long and lodged in the brush of the wall. Peering in through the door, I saw the snake's little head poking out of some branches. It looked so innocent and young and it was difficult to work out what type it was, but we gave it plenty of space, not wanting to provoke it. It flicked its tongue repeatedly, trying to work out what we were and after a time, slithered out of the hut in a flash and into the undergrowth.

'I wonder where its mummy is?' I joked.

My companion looked around uneasily.

'Not long out of the egg, that one. The nest can't be that far away,' I added, looking up and down the brush walls for further movement.

'What do you reckon it was?'

'Difficult to tell. Cobra?'

Needless to say, my companion found an alternative spot in another hut nearby and began to settle in. Gathering up some sticks and dried grass, kicking the area first to check there was nothing lurking there, I soon had a fire going which we used to boil water for our dinner. As the light began to fade, we chatted about the day and what we had seen and discussed the plans for the morning.

The day had been everything I had been dreaming of in the months before the expedition. We were in the wild, seeing remote villages and wildlife in its natural habitat and really felt 'out there'. We joked about what Andreas and the folks at Kwanda Lodge would be eating and somehow decided that it would be chicken soup followed by steak, fried potatoes, fresh vegetables and a glass of red wine. We were now on our own and having to live by our own wits. Revitalised after our own piping hot pasta mixed with instant soup, we wandered back to our respective tents to rest.

The night was cold and I was unable to settle. In the early hours I had to pull on my lightweight fleece to try to stave off the chill. I would curl up in a ball trying to retain heat but then get uncomfortable and have to change position. I bemoaned the fact that I hadn't brought a sleeping bag to snuggle into and hoped it would warm up as we approached the coast. The days were baking, reaching well over thirty-five degrees centigrade, but at night the temperature was dropping into the low single figures, making getting to sleep difficult.

We set off early in the morning and headed straight for the lake to fill our empty bottles, enjoying coffee and energy bars by the water's edge. Leaving the water and setting off north to avoid an inlet, we found a narrow path going in the direction we wanted and I took the lead to take on the navigation duties.

As we were chatting about the uncomfortable night we had both experienced, there was a massive rustle in the leaves close to our left and a huge black mamba hurriedly slithered away into the bush.

'Bloody hell!' I shouted, leaping ahead as my heart skipped a beat and the adrenalin soared.

Within seconds it was gone. The vision of the snake, with greyish scales and slim but heavy body, will stay with me forever as a moment of fright and exhilaration at the same time.

'Christ, that was close!' uttered my companion behind me in mild understatement.

I was shocked at the close encounter and glad it hadn't come towards us. Like us, the snake was probably trying to warm itself after a cold night and didn't expect people to be passing close by.

'Let's get going,' urged Chaz as he marched past me along the path. 'These things have been known to chase after people.'

Taking his word for it, I followed briskly behind, glancing nervously left and right for any other unwelcome surprises. A bit further on, I spotted what the mamba probably preyed on. Small creatures the size of a squirrel darted quickly across the ground and disappeared up nearby trees. Looking closer, they looked more like chipmunks and their coats were light brown in colour, perfect for hiding in the desiccated brush. We saw three or four of them in quick succession and wondered how long their lives would be, bearing in mind the dangers that surrounded them.

A little further on, we passed some teenagers pushing their decrepit and rusty bikes through the sand, laden with supplies. As the encounter with the snake was fresh in my mind, I tried to explain what we had seen by wriggling my arm and pointing up the path. The lad in front gave me a knowing smile and nodded his head, explaining to his friend what I had seen. I felt I had to warn them, as an encounter could be deadly, but later realised that the locals probably saw them all the time and treated them as a routine hazard of living in the bush.

The heat soared and a while later we met Joseph, who was cutting down a tree with a homemade axe. All he had with him, apart from his axe, was a plastic bottle of water placed in the shade of a tree. His dark skin glistened with the effort and he told us that he was from Zimbabwe, having left the country a decade earlier due to 'problems' there. Nearby stood a pile a neatly cut logs, evidence of the morning's toil. We told him of our encounter with the mamba and he just smiled, telling us they were everywhere.

We asked for directions to the town of Muchongeza and Joseph pointed the way, telling us it was three kilometres distant. I always took estimated distances with a pinch of salt in Mozambique, as they were often inaccurate and wildly understated, but we thanked him anyway before pressing on.

We passed through an area where the vegetation had been burned on either side of the track and was still smouldering. Thick clouds of smoke wafted towards us and we held our hands across our mouths and noses to stifle the smell. We were told later that loggers used the practice to kill and scare off the snakes so that they could take the trees undisturbed.

A few hours of following a variety of paths and about eight kilometres later, we were pleased to see a water tower shaped like a fort in the distance, signalling our arrival at the town. It was quite a large place, with smart, whitewashed official looking buildings, national flags flying, on the outer edge. As we moved deeper into town, the buildings took on a sorrier state, made primarily of mud and logs. Seeing some men chatting in the shade, we asked where we could get a drink and one of them directed us to a brick-built bar, painted in dark blue from floor to ceiling. We were hoping the drinks would be cold, having seen electric lines running into the building, but sadly they were not. Taking them gratefully anyway, we were glad to retreat from the sun.

Often I would see electricity pylons and cables snaking their way through the countryside, but arriving in small towns and villages, though cables were everywhere, the electricity just didn't materialise. I learnt later that the power created by the hydro-electric dam at Cahora Bassa was all sold to South Africa, so in northern Mozambique people often had to do without what those in the West would regard as an essential resource.

As we enjoyed our refreshment, young children wandered over and regarded us with curiosity. Initially, they would hang back and peer at us from around the building's corner, but as their courage grew, they came closer and giggled at us. I gave some biscuits to a little boy closest to me and he took them, shyly retreating out of sight. A few adults walked over and, speaking in broken English, asked us where we were going. Peering at his satnav, my companion shouted out 'Cerinde' and the men nodded their heads, pointing the way out of town.

We left the place along a well-established track which initially headed in the right direction, but after a while began to curl towards the northeast and away from the lake. Staying on the route, we hoped to find a more suitable one later, which would bring us back on course. After an hour of hard slog, we came to a village, seeking directions for Cerinde, but the locals just wafted their arms in its general direction. Spotting a path beyond the village that looked promising and in the absence of any road signs, we headed for it, keeping our fingers crossed.

Initially, the path was great, as it followed the contours of the land, but after a few kilometres it became narrower and narrower and more overgrown, until it finally disappeared altogether. We searched around desperately, to see if the track would reappear further on, but despite our best efforts, we had no luck. Checking the Sygic navigation tool on our phones, we worked out that we were about five kilometres from the lake and looked around for a route to follow. As I continued to study the on-screen map, I noticed my companion disappear through some brush and a short while later heard him shout out that he had found something. Following his steps, I came to the top of a small river bank and looked down to see him operating his compass.

'What have you got mate?' I asked.

'I reckon this stream bed will lead us down to the lake,' he proclaimed.

'Not necessarily. It might lead somewhere else.'

Chaz then began to show me the bends in the river, putting an idea forward that if we followed it in a certain direction, we would hit the lake. I wasn't convinced with his thesis though and told him so. As it was hot and we didn't want to argue, we agreed to follow it for a kilometre and if it wasn't heading towards the lake, we would come up with another plan.

After a few hundred metres, scrabbling over logs, hacking through dry bush and being clawed at by thorns, we sat down on the riverbed in the shade of a large tree for a rethink. As I had suspected, the water course was leading us away from the lake and not a viable option. Deciding to scramble out, we forced a route through the undergrowth for another hour, until we found a narrow path going in the direction we wanted.

We had been moving for a while when something hissed at us loudly from the undergrowth to our right. It was a sound I knew well, having come across puff adders in Africa on previous trips. The serpent we had disturbed causes the most fatalities from snake bites in Africa, partly due to its geographical range, but also because of his potent cytotoxic venom which causes necrosis and sometimes even gangrene. It is a slow-moving snake, preferring to wait in ambush by paths and animal trails, before striking with lightning speed and consuming its meal. I wanted to take a closer look to be sure it was a puff adder, but my friend was less keen. We set off again, leaving the serpent in peace.

Eventually, we hit a larger track and followed it parallel to the lake for a few kilometres. By now it was late in the day and we had to find somewhere to camp and collect water, which was disappearing fast again due to the heat. Taking a bearing directly south, leaving the track behind, we pushed our way through tall grasses, well over our heads. The threat from snakes was probably at the front of both our minds.

After much effort, we spotted through the vegetation a few huts on some raised ground and headed for them with renewed vigour. Dumping our packs, we congratulated ourselves on our find. The huts were abandoned and it was an excellent location, with a level surface for the tents and a view overlooking a lagoon a short distance away. It was probably another old fishing camp.

While my companion fetched some water, I made a fire from sticks and brush nearby so that we could boil water for the evening meal. As I was preparing my food, he shouted out that he had a scorpion close to his tent. The campsite wasn't as perfect as we had originally thought. Whenever I was outside the tent, I always made sure that the zip was fully done up to stop intruders from entering. Scorpions, spiders and other creatures have a habit of wandering around and seeking out dark enclosed spaces to hide. The last thing you want is to share your tent with something that shouldn't be there.

A little later, as I was settling down to sleep, I heard rustling in the dried grass close to me but couldn't work out what it was. There would be frantic activity and then it would go quiet for a few minutes before starting again. I called out to Chaz and he had heard the same, thinking they were rats or mice. Whatever it was made a racket all night by constantly scurrying around.

After a long, cold night, it was good to be up, warming my hands by the camp fire and enjoying some hot coffee as the sun began to rise. My companion strolled over and made some porridge as we chatted about the day to come. Breaking camp, we walked back to the track and headed east, savouring the first of the sun's rays before it became too hot. The going was flat and the route took us through patches of forest, followed by large open areas close to the water. It was my favourite time of the day as I felt fresh and energised, the temperature was comfortable and the adventure of a new day lay ahead.

At a water stop on a slight ridge, a few hours into the walk, we consulted our satnav as the track had begun to curl away from our desired course. After a few minutes of deliberation, Chaz pointed south towards the lake saying that was where we should go and just set off. I couldn't believe that he didn't want to discuss the route further, particularly as we had struggled with lagoons so far into the trek. Whenever we hit one, we had to walk inland for hours to get around the feature before continuing on our way. By taking a route south, we were going to come across the same problem again and it didn't make sense.

I watched and slowly shook my head as he strode off into the distance, never looking back, and at that moment knew that I was probably better on my own for the remainder of the journey. We had got on well over previous weeks and performed well as a team, but to just walk off with little discussion wasn't what I was looking for from a trekking companion, particularly in an area so fraught with danger. The act of just leaving concerned me and I knew that if he did it once he would probably do it again and I concluded that we had differing opinions on how a team should operate.

Taking a north-easterly bearing, I set off through the

brush, occasionally seeing him way in the distance to my right, but after a while he was gone. I couldn't believe that we had parted ways, when we had discussed during the planning phase the importance of staying together. We knew that we would be more vulnerable on our own, particularly if we met hostile locals, and I was disappointed that he had made both our journeys that much harder. We would both pay for the separation later in our treks.

As I walked, I reconciled myself to the fact that I would now be alone and began to relish the idea. I was confident in my own abilities, having served in extreme environments with the army, and hoped I had the skills and experience to make it to the coast.

I found a suitable path and began to think through my new situation. I was able to walk up to forty kilometres a day, as we had done in Zambia where the going was easier, and was comfortable living in the wild. I had everything I needed, although a more sophisticated navigational tool would have been preferable. The Sygic app on my phone was useful but didn't have the detail that I needed to get around the lagoons and it was often just plain wrong. It didn't show contours, vegetation, all the settlements or every track, but it was all that I had.

After an hour of steady walking through bush, the land began to dip down and I spotted an expanse of water through the trees. I had hit another huge lagoon and broke into a grin. Although I still had to get around it, my route awareness had proved correct. Wherever my friend was, he would hit the same feature, although be closer to the lake and have to make a far bigger detour. There were small ripples on the water from the gentle breeze blowing from the south and groups of waterbirds were stepping through the shallows, on the lookout for food.

The feature stretched for over five hundred metres in front of me and in a safer environment I would have considered swimming it to save time, but having seen the size of the crocodiles over previous days, I knew it wasn't an option.

The most dangerous reptile is the one you cannot see and although I couldn't spot any at that point, I knew they could be resting on the bottom, waiting for a chance to attack.

Following the twists and turns of the lagoon for a kilometre, I began to see huge crocodiles in the tangled vegetation by the shore, almost fully submerged. At one point, as I was moving through thorny scrub close to the water, one hissed at me when I got too close. I moved nearer to take a photo, but it slunk back into the water and disappeared before I could get a clear shot.

Every so often I would stop and look behind me to see if Chaz had reached the lagoon, but he was nowhere to be seen. I pushed on, the far bank becoming tantalizingly close, but every time I turned a corner there was another finger of the lagoon to circumvent. Seeing a possible route through the tall grass that would save me time, I moved towards it and stopped at the top of a small bank. As I was about to continue, I glanced downwards and saw a large green-scaled snake moving slowly just below me. It looked like a cobra, but I wasn't sure and wasn't going to take any chances. Banging the ground with my foot repeatedly, I watched the reptile quickly slither off into thicker grass and I rapidly moved through to the other side.

Further on, when I was looking for another shortcut across a boggy section and saw crocodiles basking in the mud, I noticed close to them a group of what looked like terrapins, resting on a circular mound. It was a perfect spot for them with the crocodiles nearby as protection, and I wondered what they offered in return. Slowly retracing my steps, I moved to firmer and higher ground.

I was content with my progress and seemed to be reaching the top of the lagoon when I reached a rocky outcrop next to the water and began to clamber over the huge car-sized boulders. The previous hour I had noticed these outcrops or kopjes creeping closer and closer to the water and suspected that sooner or later they would pose a challenge. Following the incline of the rocks, I found myself next to a cliff as high as a four-storey building, with cracks in the rock forming a narrow walkway, about six inches wide, along its side. The route looked passable for about a hundred metres and then it disappeared from view around a corner.

Pausing to consider my options, I took a drink of water and a deep breath. To go back and retrace my route around the kopjes and through thick undergrowth could take hours and I desperately looked around for an alternative to the one in front of me.

As I was considering my route, I saw in the distance, a few hundred metres away, a fisherman in a small dugout paddling across the water and waved my arms to attract his attention. If I could get a lift to the other side it would save me a lot of time and energy. Spotting my waves, the man looked in my direction for a few moments, but then ignored me and carried on paddling. In frustration, I edged towards the cliff for another look and convinced myself that it was worth a chance.

Moving towards the edge, I undid the belt on my pack just in case I fell into the lagoon and began to move slowly along the rock face, taking care with my handholds and placement of my feet. I had climbed in my younger days and was confident in my abilities. Below me, about thirty feet down, the water glistened in the sunlight and apart from the presence of crocodiles, would have made a perfect location for a swim.

After what seemed an age, the cliff began to disappear into thick vegetation and my progress was halted. The only way was up and after a short climb, I found myself in a flatter area overgrown with bush. Forcing my way through, I had to take off my pack as it was catching on the thorns, and slowly made my way up the slope. I was concerned about snakes again, as it was a perfect environment for them, offering places to bask and plenty of shade. I kept moving, wanting to be rid of the place.

Scrambling through the brush, as thorns tore at my skin I willed myself on, trying to find a way out of the maze.

Looking down at my hands, I saw that the thorns had punctured some of the blisters on my index fingers caused by taking anti-malarial doxycycline tablets for several weeks. Fluid was oozing out of the cuts and I had to stop for a moment to dab them and apply antiseptic cream.

I looked around at my setting. I was surrounded by short, prickly trees and dense undergrowth and the lack of paths told me that few had ventured there before. Continuing on, eventually I came to a more open flat area and made my way back to the rocky water's edge. I was at the top of the lagoon and had turned a corner. Looking far into the distance towards Lake Cahora Bassa, I could see that as long as I stayed near the water and walked on the rocks, I could progress quite well and get back on track. Thick, sloppy vegetation comprised of water hyacinth, water lilies and algae lined the water's edge as far as I could see and I knew that I had to be wary of crocodiles which could be hiding there.

As I was stepping over some boulders, a rapid movement caught my eye and I saw a lizard race down the rocks towards the water, closely followed by a thin snake with a beautiful yellow band along its length. When I moved my arm, the serpent paused, allowing the lizard to escape into a gap in the rocks.

I walked beside the water for a few hours, keeping a constant lookout, until I spotted a few huts in a small bay and made my way wearily towards them. Fishermen were repairing their nets and seemed surprised to see this dishevelled, sweaty figure approach out of the bush.

Taking out my compass and checking the satnav, I asked for directions to Cerinde and they pointed to a small path leading away from their camp through the trees. I took it and followed its winding course for a short distance until I hit water again. To my right in the distance, I saw a few huts and some goats grazing nearby and headed for it, wondering if I had found my destination.

In previous days, Chaz and I had talked about Cerinde as

some kind of nirvana, a town or at least a decent sized village with everything we would want, but what I saw fell laughably short of expectation. It consisted of three rickety mud huts, a small shed for the goats and a vegetable patch at the rear. It was now an hour from sunset and as I plodded disconsolately towards the buildings, my friend suddenly appeared and waved me in.

After greeting each other, we made our way towards the huts and I sat down heavily on a rickety stool, exhausted after the effort of the day. It was great to rest and the taste of the beer that I bought from one of the locals, although warm, was wonderful. We discussed what had happened to us during the day and I learnt that Chaz had secured the help of some locals to guide him around the lagoon.

'I think you should stay on your own, mate,' I said, taking another swig of beer, having made my mind up during the tortuous day.

'Yeah,' he replied after a few moments, looking out across the water. 'I'm going to cross the lake and make my way to Tete that way. It's easier on the southern side and I can make better progress there.'

Thinking about it later, I wondered if he had wanted to be on the southern side all along and had chosen to stick close to the water on the north shore in order to find a boat to cross over. The country was more open on the opposite bank and it was much easier and faster to travel through. On this side it was difficult to navigate and the going was tough, but I felt it was more interesting and was happy to stay. We hardly spoke as the light disappeared, we just stared out over the rippling water, deep in our own thoughts.

I put up my tent between the huts and sorted out my gear, noticing that a penny-sized hole had appeared in the material at the front of my boot. It must have been caused by the thorns during the day and I hoped it wouldn't get much worse over the coming weeks. The boots had served me well along the Camino de Santiago a few months before and I needed them to stay the distance. Sitting back down on my stool, I could tell it was going to be another cold night, as the wind began to build.

Later, when it was dark, the woman in the settlement offered me some cold nshima and a few pieces of congealed goat to eat, but I politely declined. I didn't feel like eating after such a difficult day and opted for another beer instead. Retiring to my bed shortly afterwards, I spent several hours shivering in the cold, replaying the events of the day in my mind and wondering if I had made the right decision to stay on the north shore and complete the journey on my own.

Chapter Four - Solo

Getting up early, I quickly packed away my gear and said goodbye to Chaz. He wished me luck from inside his tent, which summed up the situation perfectly and I set off looking for a path to take me east. I wouldn't see him again on the expedition. I was still a little sad to be leaving my trekking companion as we had enjoyed some good times, particularly in Zambia on the way to the border, but it was time to move on and face the wild on my own.

The narrow path twisted and turned through the undergrowth and I had a spring in my step, pleased to be following my own destiny. After a few hours, before the heat of the day really hit, the path began to head north away from my desired course and my heart sank. I wanted to handrail the lake as much as possible, not only because it was an excellent navigational aid, but it was also my most reliable source of water. Inland, many of the river and stream beds were as dry as a bone due to the season and water could only really be found in villages which were thin on the ground.

I followed the path for a further kilometre, but was not convinced that it was going to swing back east and so decided to travel across country to try to find a better route. My satnav showed there was a settlement about ten kilometres away and I headed for it, hoping that the bush wouldn't be too difficult to travel through. After a hundred metres I stopped and looked back the way I'd come and could see no sign of the path. I was heading into uncharted territory and although it was a little daunting, I was excited. It would be a good opportunity to test my navigation skills again.

The ground undulated slightly and it was difficult to see more than fifty metres ahead. The vegetation closed in around me and thorns snatched at my shirt. I came across a large dried up pond with animal tracks around it, which gave me relief from the thorns until I had to push into the scrub once more. Gradually, the vegetation began to thin a little and I could see further and began to keep a steadier course.

After about an hour of steady progress, I noticed a pale patch of sand ahead. It was the edge of a track used by light vehicles and I stumbled onto it, glad to have a definite route once more. Unfortunately, it was heading north-south, so I followed it towards the lake for a while, hoping to find a branch route to the east.

Coming over a rise, I spotted a hut in the trees and waved at the man cutting wood by his front door. Explaining to him that I wanted to head east and along the lake, he pointed back the way I had come, telling me that was the way to go. Thanking him, I followed the track for a few kilometres until it bisected a logging road and joined it.

The area I was now passing through was sparsely populated and although there were signs of humanity, there were no settlements that I could see. The track I was on had been carved through the dirt like a thick knife through freshly baked cake, appearing to me more like a scar than a thoroughfare.

Taking a break on a log a little later, I spotted a local woman dressed in loose-fitting and colourful red and yellow patterned clothes with a small child by her side. She scuttled past me uncertainly. Remaining seated, I waved to show that I was friendly, but she ignored me and increased her pace without looking back. I suppose that from her point of view, I was a strange man of a colour she would rarely have seen and she was there without friends or neighbours close by and therefore considered me a threat.

Cresting a hill a few kilometres further on, I had to stop and take in a view of devastation. Below me, stretching for some distance either side of the track, was an area that had been logged, the ground blackened by fire. Every single tree had been taken, their remnants just a foot or two of burnt trunk. It was heartbreaking to see, so much so that I wondered if the place would ever heal. Walking through the charred earth, I was met with silence, the birds and animals having fled from this place of death.

Around midday, I came to a village overlooking a floodplain and sought out the shop to buy some refreshment. An older man wearing a threadbare suit jacket and tatty trousers wandered over and introduced himself as a former 'freedom fighter'. He was originally from Zimbabwe and had come over to fight in the civil war, telling me of fierce battles in the area. I learnt later that his country had supported Frelimo by encouraging fighting age males to travel to Mozambique to oversee their own interests and protect the border between the two nations.

I asked why he was still there and he explained that he couldn't return home and had been living illegally in Mozambique for decades. Apparently, his country was reluctant to take returning fighters and actively sought them out and imprisoned those they found. He had a wife and children and grew crops nearby which he sold to loggers, and he seemed content with his lot. He wished me well when I left and pointed me towards a track that skipped around the lagoons, which would allow me to progress more quickly.

Moving through the bush some time later, I was startled with the rustle of dry leaves to my right and saw a large black snake, possibly a cobra, race off into the trees. It was probably sunning itself and I was glad that it had disappeared so quickly. In Mozambique, I was learning a new respect for snakes. I'd heard stories and read articles about the reptiles chasing after people and raising themselves off the ground to intimidate, but so far they had only raced away from me as fast as they could manage. Later that same day, when I was off the path and moving through thick scrub, another large snake, olive green in colour, dropped off a branch close to me and gave me a fright before slithering quickly away.

The vegetation around me began to thin out, until there were just small bushes and the occasional spindly tree or acacia. The soil had begun to turn a reddish colour, hinting that I was crossing into an iron rich area. In the distance, were a set of steep hills which looked ominously difficult to climb, particularly in the oppressive heat. Back in Zumbo, Chaz and

I had studied the terrain along the northern shore and had decided that it would be reasonable going, but the hills in front and to the left of me told a different story. Their tops were flat, perfect for defence and I wondered if people had settled on them in years gone by for protection.

Where the path crossed a small stream, I noticed some small girls collecting tomatoes close to a pond. Wandering over, I asked if I could buy some by showing some meticais, the local currency, and one the girls disappeared behind a large acacia and brought back a huge bowlful. Giving her some money and selecting five of the largest tomatoes, I spent the next kilometre slowly gorging myself. My particular favourites were those with some green to them, offering a firmer, although still tasty bite. Thereafter, I would look out for them in villages I passed through, as they were some of the best I had ever tasted.

In the late afternoon, the path wound its way down towards the lake and I followed it for several kilometres before cutting back into the trees. Wanting somewhere to camp for the night, I spotted huts in the distance and headed towards them through the scrub, hoping to find a suitable spot. The homes were scattered randomly around the wood and looked down through light vegetation to the lake a few hundred metres away.

Small children played with homemade toys in the dust, smiling shyly as I strolled past. I found some boys hanging around a shop and bought some 'Fizz', a soft drink I would get to know well on my journey. The drink came in a small plastic bottle in a variety of flavours and was very sweet, perfect for a long-distance trekker needing an energy boost and refreshment. Even when warm, as it invariably was, it was a pleasant change from tepid lake and river water.

A woman of about thirty came over from the hut nearby and began chatting to me about my trip, and was amazed that I would take on such a journey. Mato was from Lusaka in Zambia and told me that she bought fish from the lake, salted them and then transported them out of Mozambique, through

Zambia and on to the southern part of the Democratic Republic of Congo (DRC), some five hundred kilometres away. She would tell me more about her entrepreneurship over the coming hours and was happy for me to pitch my tent next to her hut. Seeing the state of my shirt which was covered in dust, she offered to wash it which I was grateful for. Afterwards, she laid it out on a simple rack and it was bone dry by morning.

Bringing me some hot water, she instructed me to wash, as after days in the bush I was filthy. Glancing down at my now clean hands, I was pleased to see that the rash and blisters on my index fingers had settled down and the skin was beginning to harden. I had decided to temporarily stop taking my anti-malarial pills a few days before, in order to reduce the rash and the intervention seemed to be working. It was a risk, but one that had to be taken.

As the temperature dropped, I warmed myself by her fire, boiled up some water for my dinner and was grateful for my first hot food, pasta and dried cooking sauce, in days. It was a basic diet, but it sustained me and anyway, I didn't have much choice in the matter. There were no restaurants within a hundred kilometres, little to buy from the local bancas and it wasn't practical to carry camping rations, due to their bulk and weight, on such a long journey.

Near to where I sat, David Livingstone and his party had enjoyed the bounty of the area and had shot game for meat when they required it. He recalls one incident when elephant was on the menu:

'We had the elephant's fore-foot cooked for ourselves, in native fashion. A large hole was dug in the ground, in which a fire was made; and, when the inside was thoroughly heated, the entire foot was placed in it, and covered over with hot ashes and soil. We had the foot thus cooked for breakfast next morning, and found it delicious'. (1)

As I was finishing up my dinner, my hostess asked if I wanted anything to drink and I paid one of the local lads to fetch some beer. An hour later, after it had got dark, the boy returned with bottles in his hands and a sweaty shirt.

'Crikey, where's he been?' I asked Mato, suddenly feeling guilty.

'Oh, he had to go to the next village along the lake,' she replied matter of factly. 'We don't have beer here.'

'If I knew how far he had to go, I would have stuck with coffee!'

'Don't worry about it; it isn't far.'

'If you say so,' I said, not totally convinced.

The beer was warm and frothed up when I flicked off the tops, but I wasn't complaining and grateful for the lad's efforts. After a few sips, my host turned to me and grinned.

'That is the first beer I have ever had!' she conceded.

'What, you've never had a beer before?' I said dumfounded. 'Surely you had beer in Lusaka?'

'No, never had it. My former husband was a Christian and very religious and never allowed it in the house.'

'Fair enough,' I replied. 'So how does it taste?'

'It's very good!' she said, throwing me a grin. 'I will have to take it again!'

'I hope I haven't led you astray!'

'No, you have not,' she smiled, looking into the fire.

Later, she told me more about her business. She explained that her customers in southern DRC were so desperate for the tasty fish that they paid high prices for it and demanded that she increased her quantities. At present, she transported the salted fish in old suitcases to the country and often sold out within minutes. She would then have to travel all the way back to Mozambique to replenish her stocks, before returning a month or so later. Her hard work had bought a house in Lusaka, the capital of Zambia, and was putting her three daughters through school there. She was a witty drinking companion and I was impressed with her business sense and drive and wished her luck for the future.

After it got dark and we were chatting by the fire, some boys appeared from the direction of the lake with baskets full to the brim with fish. Using the fire for light, they proceeded to gut and clean the catch, before caking them in salt and wrapping them in vines. I was impressed with their handiwork and use of a knife and Mato told me that the children near the lake learnt to handle fish from an early age, as it was a staple in their diet.

Awoken by a rooster strutting around my tent, I left early, the morning cold and misty. Mato had shown me the best route to take and I followed it for a few kilometres through the trees, before it hit a larger track. Few vehicles seemed to use the uneven tracks, wide enough for a car, but I did see small 50cc motorbikes, often piled high with boxes, beer or chickens, ridden by young locals. I would wave to them enthusiastically, noticing their heavy coats and trousers, pleased to see other living souls in the crushing heat. But many would just ignore me, eager to get on their way, save the few who gave a reluctant nod or wave. Trekking is not something people in Mozambique have much time for, where survival and getting by are the main concerns.

Arriving at a village mid-morning, I bought a drink and took a few moments in the shade. A local passing by introduced himself as Howard and offered to show me the way through the myriad of paths, so we set off into the trees. Walking with me for over a kilometre, he didn't say much, apart from greeting those we passed on the track, and was probably happy with the diversion.

When he left me, he pointed the way enthusiastically towards some distant wooded hills, smiled, turned around and headed back the way we had come. It was good to be in the shade for a while and I plodded on for the rest of the morning, choosing which path to take with care and every so often, checking my compass.

At one point I arrived at some huts, where a few women were singing to each other and pounding into tubs with thick wooden logs, presumably making cassava flour. The smell of sweat hung in the air and I didn't envy their workload in the oppressive heat. Not wishing to disturb them, I walked on and spoke to a man relaxing in the shade.

'Jussalo?' I asked, hoping for directions to the settlement I wanted to head for further along the lake.

The man shook his head and waved me away as if I had offended him.

'Jussalo?' I insisted.

Rising slowly, he stretched himself, looked me up and down and pointed to a ridge in the distance. Thanking him, I headed towards the spot, using paths that crisscrossed the crops. After a kilometre of steady progress, I began to climb an incline and found some huts at the top of a hill, chickens disappearing in panic at my approach. A man wearing a dirty white vest and carrying a kind of hoe called out to me and asked something, presumably where I was going.

'Jussalo?' I asked, pointing to the east.

'Nao,' he replied, Portuguese for 'no', shaking his head and pointing the way I had come.

'Jussalo?' I said incredulous, pointing in the same direction.

Nodding, he wandered off, presumably to his crops. I checked my compass and satnav and decided that I disagreed with the man, as he was pointing west and 180 degrees in the wrong direction. Perhaps he was having a joke at my expense, I wasn't sure, but I set out in the direction I thought was right and soon found a path that I was happy with. My route twisted through the trees, offering me occasional glimpses of the lake in the distance and I was glad of the intermittent shade, covering several kilometres with ease.

In the early afternoon, as I dropped through another forested area, I spotted water up ahead and my heart sank; I had hit another lagoon. Despite my best efforts, it seemed that every path led down to the water, rather than going around it. Following the course of the lagoon for a while, bumping into the occasional disgruntled crocodile, I realised that it didn't go as far inland as others and pressed on. Initially, the shoreline had sand and pebbles, but large rocks began to appear which I had to clamber over, slowing me down.

Rounding a corner, I came across two dugout canoes wedged in the sand, one with its bow under water, and was tempted to borrow the better craft. By the edge of the trees was a makeshift fishing camp although no one was at home. It was only a hundred metres to the other side and the boat would save me hours but I left it where it was, not wishing to incur the wrath of the owner, and stayed close to the water.

The lagoon's fingers took me backwards and forwards as I followed its edge and occasionally I would risk stepping through marshy ground to try to save some time. As I came to a rocky area, some movement in the trees nearby caught my attention and I wandered over to take a look. Glancing upwards, I initially couldn't see anything until there was movement again and I saw a vervet monkey, the size of a cat, looking down at me. Its light brown and grey fur was perfect camouflage in the dappled light of the tree. Its intelligent black face was tinged with white and its piercing eyes bore down on me. As we were studying each other, there was more movement in a tree nearby and the rest of the family came over to investigate.

As I moved from position to position to gain a better view of the creatures through the foliage, their heads would follow and when they lost sight of me, they would move to a better position to maintain a visual. Vervets are common in East Africa and usually live in groups of ten to thirty family members, spending much of the day foraging for berries and seeds. I hadn't seen many in Mozambique and wondered if they, like many of the other animals, had been decimated during the civil war when used as a food source. As they began to move off, I spotted a few young ones firmly clutching the backs of their mothers, who regarded me anxiously. Leaving them to their foraging, I strolled back to the water's edge and continued north.

Eventually, after covering a few kilometres, I reached the river mouth that flowed into the lagoon, had a drink and took stock. The curse of the lagoons was getting me down and I wondered if I would be hitting them every day. My satnav wasn't showing them clearly and I estimated that I had at least another hundred kilometres to go before hitting the dam at the eastern end of Cahora Bassa Lake. Factoring in the lagoons could easily double that distance and I worried about running out of time. The visa that I had been issued was for only one month, though it could be extended for an additional month, after which I would have to leave the country. Various options for my journey began to run through my mind, as the relentless sun beat down.

I walked on for a while and spotted a pool in an otherwise dry riverbed. It was surrounded by large boulders and I decided to strip off and take a dip to cool down, as I knew that such opportunities would probably be rare. It was far enough from the deep water of the lagoon and the threat of crocodiles, and the clear water was too much to resist. The feeling of getting my head under water was wonderful and I was able to wash away the dust and grime that had built up on the trek.

It was the first time I had felt truly relaxed in days and I savoured the moment. Despite the tranquillity, every so often I was compelled to scan the rocks and water, as I didn't want to get a nasty surprise from an unwelcome visitor. My main concern was for snakes nearby which could glide into the water with barely a ripple. They are known to be good swimmers.

Suitably refreshed, I sat on a rock to dry off and began to plan what I was going to do. Continuing east seemed to be madness because I would go on hitting lagoons, some of which took half a day to circumvent. I could push north east along the river, hope to find a track that crossed it and then move parallel with the lake to make some distance, before dropping back down to meet it further on. After some time, deep in thought and frustrated with the lagoons, I decided to follow the river inland and take my chances there.

The river was about a hundred metres across, with small pools everywhere and littered with boulders. It was the dry season and I picked my way along the river bed, wondering what it would be like in full flood. Bugs of amazing colours danced on the still water and apart from the odd mosquito, it was the perfect spot.

Glancing at the sand and mud around the pools, I noticed a myriad of tracks and prints, but one set stood out above all others. There were four impressions in the earth, showing the front digits, with a larger pad impression at the rear, the total print measuring about four inches across. They looked a little like dog footprints, only larger and I realised with apprehension that they were from a big cat, probably a leopard. Glancing nervously at the treeline, I let my eyes drift along the foliage, wondering if I was being watched.

'No, you're not there, are you?' I called out, shaking my head.

Taking another look along the far bank to put my mind at rest, shielding my eyes from the sun with my hand, I shouldered my pack and continued on. I was uneasy at the find, as I was miles into the wilderness, but reminded myself that this was what I had come for. I travelled along the river for some distance, my progress hampered by the uneven terrain, hoping to find a track crossing it, but all I saw was thick vegetation on either side with no hint of human presence.

As I came round a bend in the river, I saw a troop of baboons a short distance away, drinking from one of the pools. Most of them scattered on seeing me. One of the larger males, however, turned to face me with yellowing dagger-like teeth and held his ground. I wondered if it would charge me and felt a tingle of fear as I studied its dog-like muzzle and sinister eyes. Barking at me in annoyance for a few moments and staring me down, he soon joined his companions scuttling into the bush.

A few kilometres further on, I found a spot to camp on even ground above a large pool. After erecting my tent and sorting out my gear, I took another dip in the cooling waters. The water was only a few feet deep, but it was good to float and relax to the sound of cicadas around me.

Before making dinner, I made coffee and sat on some rocks taking in the view. I was surrounded by low rocky hills, covered in a variety of dried out trees and the sound of birds echoed along the valley. I realised again that this was what I had come for – the tranquillity, the peace, the animals, the surroundings – and relished the moment.

In the early hours, I woke with a start to a sound close by. I kept very still, trying to pick up what it was and heard something move close to the tent. It sounded like a step, followed by sniffing and I wondered if my imagination had got the better of me. Minutes passed without a sound and then I heard it again, low steady sounds of something moving slowly through the grass very close by. Keeping as quiet as I could, I reached into the belt pocket on my pack for my knife and braced myself. More time passed until eventually whatever it was moved off and all went quiet again. It took me ages to settle, but after a few hours I drifted off and slept till dawn.

The next morning dawned cold and grey and I was reluctant to rise, but after a few minutes was able to motivate myself and face the day. Scouting around my tent looking for the tracks of my visitor, I didn't find anything conclusive as the ground was rocky and hard. I wondered if a leopard had come across my tent whilst patrolling its territory, attracted by the scent. It could also have been a baboon. Either way, it had been an animal of some significance and I was thrilled, although still a little concerned at the encounter.

Being on the road for some time, you develop routines of behaviour that you become comfortable with. I had developed a routine for starting the day, for instance, not dissimilar to that of Livingstone on his Zambezi expedition:

'As a specimen of our mode of marching, we rise about five, or as soon as dawn appears, take a cup of tea and a bit of biscuit; the servants fold up the blankets and stow them away in the bags they carry...the cook secures the dishes, and all are away by sunrise. If a convenient spot can be found we halt for breakfast about nine am.' (1)

Of course, being solo at this stage I didn't have someone to help me break camp, but I was always on the road without delay. My evening routine was also straightforward and after boiling some water for my usual pasta dinner and pitching my tent, I would settle down to my meal as the sun went down, write up my diary and prepare for the night. On Livingstone's expedition, they had the additional burden of finding food before they slept and a couple of the members of the expedition would trek out of camp to hunt for game. The meat would then have to be carried back, butchered, prepared and cooked for the hungry travellers.

I set off along the riverbed in good spirits, but after a few hours still hadn't found a track crossing it. Taking a rest under some trees, I pulled out my iPhone to see if the digital map could offer a clue. Zooming in on my location with my fingers, I was hoping to see a track going eastwards that would allow me to follow the lake, but there was nothing. Zooming in even closer, I saw the faintest line indicating a path of some sort, squiggling its way north east. Following its course on screen, the track travelled for about eighty kilometres to a settlement called Fingoe and I decided to follow it, hoping to bisect another track on the way that would bring me back on course and closer to the lake.

After leaving the river and cutting across country for a few kilometres, I eventually found the path which was narrow but usable and hoped that it didn't peter out as others had done. Later, I saw bicycle tracks in the dirt and felt confident that I had found the right route. As there were no roads in this part of Mozambique, locals had to travel through the bush and their routes became footpaths over time. David Livingstone describes well what he experienced on his journey and what has probably changed little, now that I was following in some of his footsteps:

'The only roads are footpaths worn by the feet of the natives into hollows a few inches deep, and about fifteen or eighteen inches wide, winding from village to village, as if made by believers in the curved line being that of beauty.'

(1)

Looking into the distance, I saw rolling hills, and it turned out I would toil up and down them for the rest of the day. I crossed dried up stream and river beds and whenever there was a small pool I would take some water and douse my cap in it to cool my head and neck. I didn't see a soul.

Entering a village a few hours later, I saw circular huts scattered widely, their roofs made of reeds and dry grass. It felt like stepping back in time to something David Livingstone would have witnessed a hundred and fifty years before. The place was in the middle of nowhere, its only communication with the outside world being a path to the next village. There were no electric cables overhead and therefore no power and it saddened me that people lived such basic lives in a modern age. I had heard from expats living near the lake that those on the north shore were almost a forgotten people; there were few roads and limited ways for resources to reach them. Apparently, money dedicated for development was concentrated in the south, close to the capital and the seat of power. Many of the people who lived in this part of northern Mozambique didn't even speak Portuguese, the national language, but only their own tribal dialects. A lack of schools, teachers, will and resources had led to this unusual situation.

Making for the centre, I spotted a red and blue flag, with the word Renamo written on it, fluttering in the breeze. The group was one of the major players involved in the civil war and was obviously playing a role still. Renamo (Resistencia Nacional Mozambicana) is a militant organisation founded in 1975 as part of an anti-communist backlash against the country's ruling Frelimo (Mozambique Liberation Front) party. The organisation, backed by Zimbabwe and South Africa at various times, was made up of dissidents and political exiles, who wanted to seize back control from the ruling class and steer the country in a different direction.

The bloody civil war between Renamo, with its power base in the rural areas and Frelimo, formed in neighbouring

Tanzania, lasted from 1977 to 1992. Atrocities on both sides were well documented, with accounts of rape, torture, stabbings, mutilation and drowning inflicted on forces and civilians. The conflict ended in a stalemate, with neither side able to deliver a killer blow and after protracted negotiations a peace deal was finally signed.

Below the flag was an area of brushed earth, with rocks neatly placed around the edge; it was obviously a place of reverence and pride. It seemed strange to have what was in essence a village square in what looked like the middle of nowhere, but I knew that pride in one's party ran deep in Mozambique. I would see similar shrines throughout my journey along the Zambezi. There were few people about, but when I spotted a man in the distance, I walked over to him and offered a greeting.

'*Bom dia*!' I called out, 'Good day,' looking into the eyes of an older man. He looked like a former soldier despite his age, with straight back, sinewy arms and weather-beaten face. He had lived, you could tell.

'Bom dia,' he replied in a gruff tone, slowly looking me up and down.

'Have you any *agua*?' I asked, conscious that my water was running low.

'*Sim*,' he replied, slowly nodding his head.

He called to one of the huts nearby and a woman emerged, presumably his wife, wearing colourful loose-fitting clothes and a shawl wrapped around her head. She was a similar age to her husband and walked with dignity towards us. The man gave her some instructions and she led me to her hut, where some large plastic containers were sitting in the shade. As she gently poured water into my bottles, I wondered what kind of life she had led out there in the bush, probably miles from the nearest village and with what looked like very little.

Later, staggering up a slope, I reached the village of Capemba and called out to an old man with scars across his forehead. I had seen the practice of scarring in other parts of Africa, including Ethiopia, Kenya and Sudan, but this was the first time in Mozambique. Quite why it was done varies from storyteller to storyteller, but I learnt later that it usually relates to a tribe or coming of age. Livingstone also witnessed the practice and other signifying marks amongst the locals:

'The men are all marked across the nose and up the middle of the forehead, with short horizontal bars or cicatrices; and a single brass earing of two or three inches diameter, like the ancient Egyptia is worn by the men.' (1)

The man greeted me warmly and took me to the village shop, a small hut made of sticks and mud, where I enjoyed a bottle of lime Fizz and rested in the shade for a while. I also bought the man a drink which he gratefully acknowledged as he sat beside me.

'Fingoe?' I asked, pointing to the north.

'*Sim*,' replied the man, wafting his hand toward the east.

'Uh?' I signaled, not understanding his answer.

'Sim, sim,' he answered enthusiastically, explaining with his hand how the track went east for a long way and then hooked north.

I checked my satnav with this new intelligence, but it gave no clue. I checked with the man again and he was adamant, so decided to follow his advice. As we had been talking, some children had gathered near us and were playing with homemade toys, small steering wheels attached by a pole to little cars, and looked as happy as any child in the West. As they raced each other, they would turn the wheel slightly and the car would change direction in the dirt, leaving circuitous impressions on the ground. I said goodbye to my new friend, but stupidly didn't top up my water bottles when I had the chance, which I would rue for the rest of the day.

On the edge of the village, a man of middle age with stoned eyes and smelling of beer staggered out of a dwelling and approached me. Speaking rapidly, he was presumably asking what I was doing and I told him that I was trekking along the lake, mentioning Cahora Bassa several times. Walking beside me, he began firing off questions agitatedly, to which I either gave a response or simply shrugged my shoulders.

After a few minutes, not content with my responses, he raised his voice and asked repeatedly for 'Documento' which I took to mean documents. I smiled broadly and carried on, not wanting to give him anything, and he began shouting and even grabbed my arm. Shaking him off, waving him away and admonishing him as a teacher would to a child, I increased my pace and walked off into the dust.

I followed the path over the hills this way and that for hours and began to worry about my diminishing water. The villages had disappeared and when I did bump into the occasional local on the track and asked where I might find some, they simply pointed off into the distance, unable to tell me how far.

Passing a small herd of cows, thin from the parched vegetation, I waved to the boy looking after them, who simply nodded, unwilling to expend further energy in the sapping heat.

'Agua?' I asked the boy after I had strolled over to him.

'Nao,' he replied, shaking his head.

'No agua,' I conceded. 'Agua that way?' I asked, pointing in the direction I was going.

'Nao,' replied my talkative friend, returning to his cows.

'Thanks for your help,' I muttered sarcastically as I rejoined the path.

Incidents like that saddened me in Mozambique. The boy obviously knew that I was asking for water, but didn't feel able to help. I wondered if there was a stream or pond nearby that he was saving for his animals, not willing to share it with a passing stranger. Even if he had wafted his hand along the track, giving me hope that there was water to come, I would have been grateful. Irritated, I pressed on.

Later, as I was passing through a wooded area, I saw a motorbike on the track coming slowly towards me and waved it down. My dwindling water supply was worrying me and I was going to ask the rider if he knew where I could find some. Apparently spooked by my appearance and gesture, he turned his bike off the path and accelerated through thick bush around me, to rejoin it further on. The figure, wearing a full-face helmet and gripping his handlebars, then stopped and glanced over his shoulder at me. I shouted to him if he knew where any 'agua' was, but he just glared as his bike slowly turned over. Waving, I headed away and pondered over the strange encounter.

The day wore on and parched and tired I eventually came down a hill towards a large, dry river bed about twenty metres across and could hear children playing noisily nearby. I saw a man standing on the far shore and walked over to him asking if there was water. Pointing to spot, he showed me where the locals had dug out the sand to create a bowl of water. David Livingstone mentioned the practice, stating that the women scraped holes in the sandbanks which allowed water to filter through, rather than taking it from the limpid river nearby. He surmised that they did it because the main stream was dirty and unhealthy during certain seasons.

I was totally dehydrated and drank my fill until I could take no more and vowed never to cut it so fine again. I had walked over forty kilometres in blistering heat over rough terrain and I was exhausted.

Once I was sated I asked the man, through words and gestures, if there was a village nearby where I could stay. I was quite happy sleeping in the wild, but I was hoping to perhaps buy a chicken for dinner and observe some more village life. Understanding my request, the man nodded and beckoned for me to follow him up the bank and along a path into the bush. He walked quickly and with my backpack and tired legs, I had to call after him a few times to slow down.

We travelled up hills, down slopes and across a streambed, but after a few kilometres I still had no sight of the settlement. Unwilling to walk further, I asked my guide how far away the village was, but he just pointed into the distance and beckoned me to follow. I went on for another five minutes, but still seeing no sign of a village, I called out to the man that I was heading back to the river. I didn't know whether it was one kilometre to go or ten, but it had been a long day and I didn't wish to prolong it. Thanking my guide, I tried to explain my thoughts, but he just stood there uncomprehending, so I turned around and retraced my steps back to the river.

After setting up camp on a bank above the river, drinking a lot more water and having something to eat, I crawled into my tent to have a final look at my satnav. Checking the screen, I couldn't find any suitable tracks heading east or even back to the lake and not wanting to return to the lagoons, resigned myself to head for Fingoe, forty kilometres away. I could see that the town was on a main road which led, albeit by a circuitous route, to my halfway point of Tete. Despite my tiredness, I hardly slept as it was bitterly cold, the ground was rock hard and I resorted to curling up in a ball waiting for dawn to come.

Setting off in the cool of the morning, I made good progress over the hills, covering some useful distance. Entering a village late in the morning, I saw tables set up under some trees, with what looked like mosquito nets on them, watched over by NGO-type workers, all wearing matching yellow T-shirts. Behind, next to the ubiquitous white off-road vehicles seen in many parts of Africa, were posters in simple cartoon format explaining the hazards of malaria, helping to get the message across about this deadly disease. It was good to see that help was being offered to some of the poorest in Mozambican society, but I wondered how wide the help was being spread. Not many people were collecting the nets, so either the message wasn't getting through, or I guessed there was an allowance for each family which had already been used up.

I had almost passed through the strung-out village when a youth darted past me, ran a few paces and then stood in my path. Gathered behind him within seconds were a few of his younger friends. With folded arms like a sumo wrestler and wearing a faded Sylvester Stallone T-shirt, I wasn't quite sure why he was in my way, but someone had sent him there for a reason.

'What's this then?' I smiled, glancing at the youth who looked almost comical with his puffed-out chest and unusual stance.

He jerked his head to the side, indicating some adults who beckoned me to them, and I strolled over, wondering what I was going to endure this time. It appeared they wanted to speak with me, as a white man passing through their village obviously drew questions. Gesturing for me to sit on a bench in the shade, they called a teacher who came and sat down next to me.

By now, there were about fifteen men, some sitting, some standing, all very much focused on me. Their looks were serious and I felt uncomfortable under their gaze. The youths who had stopped me on the road were hanging back at the rear. The teacher, in broken English, asked me what I was doing there and my response about my journey was passed on to the others. I explained my progress from Zumbo and that I was on my way along the lake towards Songo, a town at its eastern end. More questions were asked and one of the older participants raised his voice, wagged his finger and looking at me sternly at my presence in the village.

This went on for several minutes, with questions being fired at me in quick succession, until the teacher said, 'The problem is….' and I guessed at that point I was going to have difficulties. He told me that the group wanted to see my papers and permission to travel. Not wanting an argument and knowing that I was in a corner, I showed them my passport. Pointing at the document being leafed through by one of the questioners, I explained that my visa was my permission to travel and I had every right to pass through the village. The teacher, agreeing with me and nodding his head, communicated this to the group and there were murmurs of acknowledgment. Then there was another question, translated through the teacher, which took me by surprise.

'Are you working in the crocodile skin trade, down by the

lake?'

'No,' I replied, shaking my head.

'Because that would be bad. The people along the lake are against it!'

'I can see why. I don't know where the factory is.'

I had thought that the locals would be pleased that the reptiles were being culled, providing them with employment in the process. Apparently not; although thinking about it later, I realised they were probably more concerned about Europeans profiting from the trade than any thoughts they had for the crocodiles. I had learnt earlier in my trip that a few top fashion houses had based themselves along the lake and used the skins for fancy items to be sold around the world.

After still further questions the mood lifted, smiles appeared, we shook hands and I walked off before they changed their minds about me being there. There was obviously a mistrust of strangers in parts of the country, and locals felt it was their right to stop and question those who raised suspicion. I put it down to Mozambique's traumatised past, from the days when Arab slavers had passed along the Zambezi with their human cargo, up until the time when white mercenaries from South Africa had fought for Renamo in the area during the civil war – plus the logging companies today.

The trek seemed to go on forever and I began to wilt, stopping regularly to rehydrate. I came across the occasional local on the track and would ask how far it was to Fingoe, but their responses weren't believable. I was in the middle of nowhere, in rolling countryside that was bland and never changed, summed up by David Livingstone when travelling with his companions in the same area:

'Our path leads frequently through vast expanses of apparently solitary scenery; a strange stillness pervades the air; no sound is heard from bird or beast or living thing; no village is near; the air is still, and earth and sky have sunk into a deep, sultry repose, and like a lonely ship on the desert sea is the long winding line of weary travellers on the hot, glaring plain.' (1)

Looking at the size of Fingoe on my satnav, I began to fantasize about the clean sheets I was going to slide under, the hot shower I was going to take and the food I was going to enjoy and a spring appeared in my step. Even though it was another forty kilometre day, the town was a real prize to aim for and I pushed myself hard to reach it.

Passing a man and his small son coming the other way a little later, I thought about how they wore no hats, no sunglasses and most likely no sun screen, and wondered what damage was being done. I had quality glasses, a sunblocking cap with legionnaire-style neck protector and had smeared high factor cream onto my hands and the exposed parts of my face. Travelling in such hot weather made it essential equipment for mzungus.

Coming over a ridge, I saw the first signs of Fingoe late in the afternoon. As I got closer, I lowered my expectations on what I might find. There were a few large buildings, one that looked like a hospital, but the majority of smaller dwellings looked shabby and small. The smoke from multiple cooking fires rose languidly through the air, giving the impression of a cloud over the town.

Trudging in, I noticed that the tarmac on the main road was cracked and uneven, with potholes everywhere, even though this was the major route in the north-western part of the country and was used to transport goods where they were needed. Fingoe has large gold deposits in the surrounding hills, mined by South African companies, but you wouldn't have guessed it judging by the rundown state of the town. It didn't look like much of the money was filtering down to the local economy.

Seeing a mechanic in a repair shop I enquired about rooms and was directed to a compound about a kilometre away. I had endured another long day and didn't want to waste energy looking for somewhere to sleep.

Arriving at the place, I saw a padlock on the front gate

and wondered if the trip had been for nothing. Calling through the gaps in the corrugated iron, I got no response, only the sight of some washing drying on a line. A woman operating a stall across the road came over to me and, pointing at the gate, asked if I wanted to stay there. She called someone on the phone and after a few minutes a man arrived on a bicycle, looking as though he had won the jackpot.

Leading me into the compound, the man walked me over to one of four steel doors in a row and fished around his pocket for a key. Finally he opened the door, and I caught a glimpse of the room that looked more like a prison cell as he began to clean. There were no windows, and unwashed, wrinkled sheets were heaped on the bed. A layer of dust on the floor indicated that it hadn't seen a brush in a long time. The smell in the room wasn't something I could put my finger on, but it wasn't pleasant. I was filthy from living in the bush for days and wasn't expecting five-star luxury, but the place didn't look fit for human habitation.

Thinking that things could only get better, I asked the man where I could wash and he led me outside around the corner, past a huge hole in the ground partly filled with stagnant water. I recoiled when he showed me the bathroom, which had no light, no mirror, no water, what looked like mud on the floor and a stink of urine and waste. Trying not to choke, I thanked him but said that I was going to look for somewhere else. I would be happier sleeping in my tent.

Walking dejectedly and slowly back into town and buying some lukewarm fritters on the way, I asked around if there was anywhere else to stay. There were few signs on the buildings, none of which mentioned rooms to let, and I was feeling a little despondent until I met a local on the street who led me to a gate set back from the road.

'Is this it?' I asked, incredulous, looking at the entrance made from more rusting corrugated iron, with weeds growing along the bottom.

I began to think that I would be sleeping in the bush after all, as the man nodded his head in response, pushed open the gate and led me inside. There was a reception hut with no one in it. As we wandered through the compound I saw a few whitewashed one-storey buildings with washing hanging up on lines. At the rear of the buildings, we found some women cooking over a fire and the man spoke to them about a room.

Reluctantly, one of them stopped what she was doing and walked me to one of the doors which she unlocked to show me inside. The man who had helped me chuckled for some reason and I thanked him as he disappeared back into the gathering gloom. There was a bed, with a blanket and mosquito net hanging over it, electric sockets to charge my phone and a bathroom with no running water. The plastic flooring was faded and torn and the mesh on the windows had holes large enough for a bird to fly through, but it was decent enough and felt like home, at least for now.

Thanking the woman, I placed my pack against the wall, sat on the bed and let out a deep sigh. If I hadn't found a place to stay, I would have had to hit the road again and sleep out, something I was happy to do, but after a tough few days felt that I deserved a bed.

After I had cleaned myself up using the bucket of cold water in the bathroom, I wandered back into town looking for something to eat. It was now dark and passing the small shops by the roadside, lit by dangling single bulbs, I could hear pop music playing on transistor radios, while locals sat on chairs outside watching me with interest. The smell of charcoal fires hinting of evening meals drifted slowly across the road and I could hear the faint laughter of children playing nearby.

In a run-down 'restaurant' close to the market, a boy served me cold fish, cold rice and cold beans and even though I was hungry, I hardly touched the food. He assured me that they also served breakfast. I paid him and trudged disconsolately back to my lodgings, praying for better luck the following day. There was at least a weak Wi-Fi signal in the room and after checking messages and reading the world headlines, I slumped into bed and quickly fell into a deep sleep.

Despite my disappointment in the town, I decided to take a rest day as I knew there wouldn't be much opportunity for renting rooms on the way to Tete. I washed my tent and boots and got one of the women living in the compound to scrub my clothes which were grey with dust.

Feeling ravenous, I wandered over in my second set of trekking gear to what looked like a restaurant on the other side of a football field. The Banco Planatara De Maria turned out to be a real find and after a breakfast of fried chicken and potatoes, I felt better again. It was another baking hot day and I enjoyed relaxing in the shade of a baobab tree rather than trekking through the bush.

I spent the day resting, eating and recharging my batteries so I'd be ready to hit the road the following day. Tete was well over 200 kilometres away and I knew it would be a slog to get there and get back on track. I tried to get my sleeping mat fixed at a motorbike shop but despite putting a number of bike repair patches on it, the mat refused to inflate and I was stuck with it.

Wandering over to the market, set out on a wide track on a slight incline in between one storey shacks, I saw women sitting on stools selling their wares laid out on plastic sheets. Tomatoes, lemons, onions, cabbages, potatoes and what looked like river weeds were laid out in the sun, waiting for a passing customer. Occasionally, the women would surreptitiously sprinkle water over their offerings, when the few potential customers were out of view, in a vain attempt to keep them moist and looking their best. Further along were baskets of kapenta, small fish the size of an AA battery, which had been dried out in the sun. This regional whitebait had come from Cahora Bassa Lake and was a staple for many families. I grew to like them when there was little else available.

As I was watching the women, a figure on homemade crutches moving behind them caught my eye, his unhurried steps ignored by those around him. His right leg ended by the knee and the ragged trouser had been fashioned to cover the skin. I wondered if the man, suitably aged to have fought in the civil war, was a landmine victim, lucky to have survived the battle but left with the consequence of war till the end of his days. I studied him as he progressed up the slope, concentrating hard where he placed the poles and felt sorry for his plight and what had become of his life. Perhaps he had a wife or family to look after him and his days were filled with happiness, but his look betrayed my optimism as he disappeared from view?

Local market in Fingoe

Knowing that I needed to leave early the next day, I strolled back to the compound office to pay for my room. The bulky man sitting behind the large metal desk smiled broadly at me and began to make his calculations, which surprised me as the price had already been agreed with the woman who had given me the key the night before. After tapping away on his calculator for several minutes, the bill was produced on a slip of paper.

'That's not right!' I said to the man, studying it and shaking my head. The cost was four times what had been agreed.

'Cost of room for two nights,' he argued in broken English.

Continuing to shake my head with a smile on my face, I told him that it was too much. The woman who I had negotiated with was called and she had a lengthy and heated discussion with the man, who eventually agreed with the original price. I wasn't sure if I had witnessed dishonesty or incompetence, but it left a bad taste in the mouth. Talking to long term expats in the country further into my journey, I decided that it was probably the former. I was informed that white people were often seen as fair game and exploited whenever an opportunity presented itself.

In the evening, I returned to the restaurant across the football field, to be told there was no food. I looked around for help. A stocky man called Felix who spoke a little English told me they had run out of most things, but after conferring with one of the female cooks, added they could offer a plate of fried eggs with rice. I readily accepted. When it came, it was just what the doctor ordered and helped to pad out my ever-pronounced ribs. Weeks of trekking over hill and dale under the African sun and on a meagre diet, had slimmed me down and I could almost feel the weight dropping off me as each day passed. Felix, who lived in Tete but was staying in Fingoe for a few days, was a logger who cut wood for the Chinese. After some good conversation and a few beers, he offered his help if I needed it when I reached Tete.

I slept well again, comfortable in a bed rather than on a cold, earthen floor. When I woke the next day though, my stomach felt strange and within minutes I was racing for the bathroom. Maybe the eggs weren't so good after all.

Chapter Five - Unusual Encounters

Leaving town I walked past the hospital, which was a modern looking place, whose one storey buildings sprawled over a few acres. Unfortunately, the gates were boarded up with thick weeds growing under and around them, and nobody was going in or out. It seemed strange and a little sad to build a facility that was obviously needed in the town and then not make it operational.

As I walked away, I wondered what locals did when they became ill; probably suffer in silence at home as they had always done. By the side of the road were scruffy, small, brick-built houses and the residents, sitting on white plastic chairs, would sometimes wave to me and ask how I was doing. I would smile back, telling them my next stop was Tete and pointing to the east. Their look would often change to surprise and as I left them I would often hear chuckles and laughter.

The broken tarmac of the town soon reverted to hard packed soil and after an hour of rolling hills, I came to a triangular monument where the track branched into two. A rough painting of a bearded soldier with a rifle over one arm and holding up a document was sketched in bright colours on to the flat surface. It looked revolutionary in design, like something you would find in Cuba.

The turning to the south was signposted to Tete, which I knew was about two hundred and fifty kilometres away, and a smart constructor's sign nearby stated the new road would be completed by the end of 2016. That was eight months ago, but I had my doubts that it was finished. Completion dates for construction projects in Africa are known to be wildly optimistic and I didn't think Mozambique would be any different. My satnav showed the start of the new road and then it petered out in the mountains down towards Cahora Bassa Dam.

Not wanting to risk losing time, I stayed on the original

track and headed for Oliveira, my end point for the day, over thirty kilometres away and a logical stopping point on my journey.

Soon afterwards, as I was passing a school with children playing in the expansive yard, a teacher called me over and asked in English where I was going. I told her about my trip and what I had experienced so far and she clutched her hands to her face.

'You are very brave!' she shrieked, beckoning some children over to her.

'I wouldn't say that,' I replied. 'It's more about exploring and finding what's out there.'

'I shall tell the school about your journey and where you are going. I will also pray for you.'

I hadn't seen much evidence of religion so far in Mozambique and wondered which faith she followed. I knew the country was primarily Christian in nature, but with Islam in evidence closer to the coast. When Chaz and I had been trekking through Zambia, we would see a church every few hours, often on the outskirts of settlements and villages. Christianity was dominant there, although the denominations varied widely, due to the strong influence of American religious charities.

Thanking the teacher, I waved to the children around her and strolled back to the track. There were few vehicles around, apart from the odd minibus or car, but I soon became accustomed to being covered in a fine silt when the logging trucks went past. The silt would find its way into my eyes, ears and up my nose and became embedded in my clothes, and only a good wash would shift it. These huge vehicles thundered along the tracks, weighed down by their load of logs on route to China.

I stopped for a break under a baobab tree and pulled off my pack for a makeshift seat. Everything around me was quiet and still and I felt completely alone, as if every living thing was resting in the shade like me. It was peaceful and calm and as I looked across the seemingly endless savannah, probably unchanged in millennia, I wondered what it would look like in future years.

The road undulated and remained in a straight line for much of the way as I crossed many river beds, most of them parched like me. There were no settlements to capture my interest or satisfy my hunger and the noise of my steps echoed in the silence.

Later, as I strolled along past a patch of thick vegetation, there was a rustle of bushes and a deer-like animal raced out onto the track, swiftly followed by a calf. It happened so fast that I only caught a glimpse, but the light brown fur and distinctive thin white stripes down their sides indicated that they were nyala. They had probably been resting in the shade when they heard my footsteps and bolted in fear. I heard their movement in the bush on the far side for barely a few seconds and then it went quiet. It was a wonderful encounter and I guessed they were there due to the remoteness of the area.

Walking into Olivera after a day in the sun, I saw that it was a plain looking place, consisting of simple brick houses interspersed with mud huts, spread out along the road. There were a few electric cables and I headed for the shop, bought a cold drink and slumped down in a chair in the corner to rest.

Asking the shop owner where I might stay, a young man called Winston was called to help in the translation. He was from Malawi and was working with his brother to find the best trees to cut for the Chinese. I asked him where I could find some food and we set out to look for some but initially could find only cold fish and nshima. Searching a little harder, we found a stall selling freshly fried potatoes with cabbage and I asked my new friend to join me. A bottle of vinegar appeared on the table, which I poured liberally on my food, making it taste even better.

I had seen a church set back from the road on the way into town, and Winston and I went over to see if I could sleep in the grounds. The priest was away and his wife, surrounded by small children clutching at her dress, told us that she couldn't give permission for me to stay but that I had to seek consent from what sounded like the 'Chief'. As she began to give directions to his house, it seemed that it was a fair distance away and I indicated to Winston that I didn't want to expend more energy looking for the man.

Thanking the woman, we walked away and my new friend told me that I could camp next to where he was living with his brother. It was a basic brick structure, covered in chipped lime green paint and the size of a large shed, with the outside toilet surrounded by a vine fence at the rear. I found a pitch to the side of the house, where the ground was like concrete and I bent a few tent pegs trying to get my shelter stable. The evening was cooling rapidly and I was kindly given a sheet to wrap myself up in, which provided a semblance of warmth during the long night.

A chorus of dogs barking till the early hours in what sounded like running battles with each other kept me awake and I was glad when morning eventually arrived and was able to warm myself by a fire next to the house. Unable to find anything for breakfast, I left town with my tummy rumbling and aimed to find something on the way.

As I walked into the rapidly bright morning, the scenery began to change and I became surrounded by kopjes left and right. Some of these formations of dark grey stone towered over a hundred metres into the sky with almost sheer rock faces and I wondered if they had ever been climbed. The sandy track stretched for miles into the distance, surrounded on both sides by thick scrub and trees. I passed through police checkpoints, stones laid out across the track to control traffic, and was waved through by bored looking officers. I never learnt why they were there.

Later, when I stopped for a drink by the side of the road, a pitiful dog with a broken leg staggered past. I threw it a biscuit, which it sniffed at suspiciously before taking it in its mouth and slinking away. The dogs that I had seen in Mozambique, half the size of normal canines and many with scars or mange, led tough lives, having to look after themselves and find food where they could.

Small trucks loaded with people or goods stopped next to me on a few occasions and asked if I wanted a lift, but I politely declined, telling them I had to go by foot. The drivers would smile and shake their heads, no doubt wondering if I had a screw loose. The road went up and down, across small bridges, and I saw three or four trucks broken down by the side of the road. Invariably, the drivers were cooking a meal in the shade, smiling away and waiting for help to arrive.

In the heat of the afternoon, miles from anywhere, I looked up and was shocked to see two men with what looked like homemade axes a short distance away. Wiping the sweat and grit out of my eyes to confirm the sight, I glanced up again and they were gone. They were probably illegal loggers, surprised to see anyone there, and had simply melted back into the bush.

When I began looking for somewhere to spend the night, a truck passed me and stopped. The driver, who spoke English, was worried about me and asked if I wanted a lift, but I told him he was going in the wrong direction and that I had to continue east. I asked if there was a village nearby and he told me there was, called Nhamatemba, a few kilometres away. I was hoping to procure a chicken or some fish and although happy to camp in the wild, I wanted to experience more of the village life that I had already witnessed.

Approaching the village, I saw huts on the hillside, partially hidden by trees, with children playing. Sitting down by the small banca, with a fizzy drink in my hand and weary from the day, I asked one of the men if I could put my tent up and he agreed, pointing to patch of ground nearby. A few minutes later, after a brief conversation with the other villagers he returned, introduced himself as Ewas and pointed to a small hut next to where I would have pitched. They had obviously been discussing whether to give me the hut or not. As I thanked him, he began to brush the place out and then laid vine mats on the floor and later brought me a blanket. It was a basic dwelling, the size of a garden shed, made of branches and dried mud and had a simple thatched roof. I felt I had landed on my feet and was grateful that people who had so little displayed such kindness.

Once I had settled in, I checked my feet which were more tender than usual and pulling off my socks, saw that there was redness around some of the toes, but thankfully no blisters. The road had been quite rocky in parts during the day and I put it down to the change in surface.

As I emerged from my hut, the man noticed me and brought over a bowl of hot water, which I used to wash away the dust. Wandering over to some villagers perched on a log, I asked if I could buy some food and flapped my arms, imitating a chicken. The group all laughed and one was brought, the price agreed and then it was dispatched and salted in front of me and cooked by one of the women on hot coals nearby. She was cooking nshima for the men, which looked like gruel, slowly stirring the meal to prevent it from burning.

My food was chewy but tasted fabulous as I sat by the fire with my hosts, and I was keen to hand out pieces of chicken to them to show my appreciation. I wondered how often they themselves ate meat and realised with sadness that nshima probably formed the main part of their diet. One of the village dogs kept creeping closer to me as I ate, attracted by the smell of the meat and much to the amusement of the villagers, but it had to make do with a few bones at the end of the meal.

After a restful night, some hot water was brought to my hut and I marveled again at the treatment I was receiving. These were poor people who knew nothing about me and yet they had gone out of their way to make me feel welcome.

Thanking my hosts for their hospitality, I hit the road under an overcast morning that would turn into a baking oven in a few hours. I crossed a large bridge over the River Capoche after a few hours and took a rest, noticing that apart from a few ponds, it was dry. In the wet season, a few months off, torrents would rage beneath where I sat, as the water forced its way towards the Zambezi.

Later, when I was thirsty and needing a break, I walked over to a stall under some trees and asked the young guy standing next to it for a *cerveja* (beer). I had tried the local brew in Mozambique a few times and had found it to be a real boost, particularly in the heat of the day when my energy levels were dipping. Wanting to know what type he had, I asked him to show me the label, but he just held the bottle tight and I couldn't see it in the gloom. I asked again by pointing at the bottle and he just shouted a price, louder than before.

Deciding to try somewhere else down the road, I walked off but the man followed me with the bottle, shouting in Portuguese. He stayed with me for a few kilometres, but never made the sale. I found another shop further on and bought what I had been craving earlier. A few men of the village were drinking gin from small bottles under a raggedy porch and we exchanged pleasantries while the drink took effect.

Crossing one of the many tributaries that flow into the Zambezi, on the way to Tete

As the road wound across country, I passed more wonderful rock formations, most with jagged tops and covered in vegetation. They were so spectacular that I had to stop and admire them for a moment and capture a few photographs.

At another village, I met Nixon, who was from Malawi and had married a local woman. We chatted in the shade and he told me about the next town called Machize, which sounded like heaven. There were restaurants, bars, laundries, rooms, you name it, everything was there, he told me. I couldn't wait.

On my way there, the track that I had been on joined a tarmac road, connecting Tete with the Zambian border, over a hundred kilometres to the north. As overloaded trucks and minibuses roared past me, it signaled a change and felt like re-entering civilisation.

Sadly, Machize didn't live up to expectations and I wandered along the strip of huts by the road, music blaring out of the windows, looking for something to eat. There was very little, apart from fizzy drinks and a fly-covered dead goat hanging outside a butcher's shop. It was obviously quite an important place, although small, with radio masts and a few government-type buildings, but it had a rough edge to it with young shirtless men swaggering about that made me uncomfortable.

Spotting a small hospital on the other side of the road, I approached, hoping to camp on the waste ground at the rear. It really was waste ground, with building materials scattered around and plastic bags caught on bushes, flapping in the breeze. A nurse in civilian clothes, seemingly offended by my request to camp, informed me in broken English that it was a place of cleanliness, as goats ran about dropping pellets on the ground. Turning my gaze towards the goats and then back at the woman, she understood the point I was making.

I walked dejectedly through the rest of town. I had been walking for nine hours and really needed to take the weight off my feet and find somewhere to rest. All I saw were more simple stalls and rundown houses, but nowhere suitable to stay.

Leaving the place and crossing a new bridge over the river Muangadeze, I spotted a sign above a building in the distance on the edge of town, hoping it was a restaurant. On reaching it I removed my pack and taking a seat, I asked the waitress what she had and she began to explain the meals in Portuguese. Not understanding a word, I asked her to show me and she led me outside and around to the kitchen. What I found was in a sorry state: congealed chicken that looked days old at the bottom of a bucket and bits of fish and scales in another. Cold chips sat forlornly in a pan close by. Not wanting to get sick again, I asked her to make me some hot chips and settled down to watch the football on a TV hanging from the wall, and enjoyed a moment of rest. There were few other diners, but those I saw were having the chicken and fish I had just seen and I felt for them.

Darkness fell soon. I was comfortable eating my meal and enjoying the football, and reluctant to leave the warmth and safety of the restaurant. Time moved on, until I forced myself out and trudged off into the night. There were no streetlights or passing cars and all I had to keep me company were the chirping cicadas out in the darkness. A few kilometres down the road I found a spot with my torch that looked promising and after checking for snakes and erecting my tent, I rolled out my liner and prepared for bed.

Waking a few hours before first light, I heard something moving close to my tent, but relaxed when it sounded like wild pigs shuffling past. One or two of the beasts seemed to stop to investigate my sleeping spot, but after a few quiet oinks and brushing a guy rope, soon lost interest and disappeared into the scrub. Leaving my campsite as dawn was breaking, I retraced my steps back to the road and turned towards Tete, still a long way away.

After walking for an hour, there was a sudden rustle of leaves to the side of me and a long black snake, probably a cobra, slithered quickly across the road and disappeared into vegetation on the other side. I was no longer surprised to see them, particularly when no habitation was near, and remained thankful that they wanted to get away from me as fast as possible.

Arriving at a big bridge over the River Luia a few hours later, I saw women washing their clothes in the trickle and laying them out neatly in the sun to dry. Waving to them, I heard shrieks of laughter from down below and was pleased that I had caused a distraction from their tedium. I stopped a few times at shacks to rest and grab a soft drink and was amazed again that the liquid was warm when there were so many electricity cables running overhead. At a village a few hours on, I came upon armed police guarding the road and watching with suspicion the approaching vehicles. They waved me on. I stopped at a hut selling fried potatoes with cabbage and gorged on a plateful before stepping back onto the road.

As I progressed, the scenery began to change again and became flatter, although still with dome-shaped kopjes close to the road. I passed a large timber yard surrounded by fencing, with hundreds of tree trunks stacked up in rows waiting to be shipped. Over twenty trucks were parked nearby, some being serviced, highlighting the scale of the logging problem. Mozambique is being deforested at a rapid, unsustainable rate and the politicians seem unwilling or powerless to stop it. I had already seen the damage caused by the logging close to Cahora Bassa Lake, where some of the best trees were located. When you consider that the trees take hundreds of years to grow to reach substantial height, you begin to understand that sizeable open spaces will be a feature of Mozambique's forests for many years to come.

A little further along the road a car passed me, turned around and the driver signaled me over. He was Chinese and speaking in reasonable English told me that he had seen me a few days earlier and was interested in what I was doing. I told him that I was trekking to the ocean, and he seemed genuinely impressed by the scale of my journey. Assuming that he was in the logging trade, I asked if he enjoyed working in Mozambique and he smiled shyly, saying he would rather be at home with his young family. Knowing that I had to press on, I said goodbye. The man offered me some money to help with the trip, but I politely declined.

Now that I was on the rough tarmac I was making better progress, even though it didn't always seem so and was tough on the feet. There were times when I would turn a corner or crest a hill and the straight road seemed to stretch on forever in front of me without a car or person to be seen. I had to dig deep and crunch through the distance.

An hour before sunset, I began to look for somewhere to stay and wandered into a village. One of the older men of the settlement, called Joseph, seemed happy to see me and walked me over to a hut next to his own place. His son, instructed to clean the place up, didn't look too impressed at my arrival, but I thanked him anyway. It was built of mud and sticks, with squared off angles and a dried grass roof and inside, there were buckets, sacks and pieces of wood. It was obviously used for storage, but I was grateful to have it as my home for the night.

The one thing that worried me though was the rickety door, held in place by some upturned screws, with an inch gap to the floor. The bush was only metres away, where all manner of creatures would live. Scorpions in particular could easily pass under the door, which was a worry and not one that I had when sleeping in my tent, protected by mesh and nylon. When researching the trip, I had learnt that these scorpions, a number of them deadly, were rife in the country and locals were often stung.

After a quick wash, I took some photos of the local children, who although were nervous of me to begin with, became excited when they looked at their image on screen. Many would never own a camera, which I thought was sad, as all their memories would fade over time. I would take a photo of a group and show them and they would climb over each other and shriek with laughter when they caught a view of themselves. As their confidence grew, they began to strike funny poses and pulled faces at the camera, which had them in fits of laughter when reviewing the images.

That evening I took another look at my shoes. The hole on one of them was getting bigger, about the size of a pound coin, and I hoped they would last until the end of the trip. As I was sorting out my gear and preparing for bed in my hut, a sudden movement caught my eye. I thought it must be a scorpion or lizard, but shining my torch into the corner I spotted a mouse scampering away. Later, when I used my torch again, the mouse just looked at me unmoved as it munched on a kernel. The tiny creature, termed 'rato' by my hosts the next day, which I learnt later was the Portuguese word for it, ran along the side of the wall for much of the night and it was difficult to settle.

Leaving early the following morning, I set off into the cool of the day. It was another straight road that disappeared into the distance below some hills, their uneven edges like a row of broken teeth. The acacia trees by the roadside added a welcome touch. Men in old suits on ancient bicycles rode gently past, and young girls with bundles of sticks on their heads eyed me with interest.

Arriving at the town of Manje a few hours later, I stopped at a water pump on the outskirts. The women, on seeing my approach, just stopped what they were doing and stared, with some of the younger children running off into the bushes. Bright yellow plastic containers were lined up neatly by the pump, reminding me what a daily chore it was to provide such a vital resource. The women would lift the containers on to their heads without complaining and head off home along the road, perhaps several kilometres away. One of the women beckoned me forward and worked the pump for me to take water, whilst the others giggled and watched on in amusement. Smiling, I put the bottle back into my side pocket and returned to the road, the ladies chattering excitedly amongst themselves as I left.

Local children posing in front of a hut I was given to sleep in

I covered the miles quickly and felt good. Passing a bustling bus stop, I caught sight of what looked like badges on the terracotta wall of a kind of waiting room, and wandered over to see what they were. A line of English football club insignia were meticulously painted in vibrant colours: Liverpool, Arsenal, Manchester United, Chelsea and a few others were immortalised in this backwater of Mozambique and it resonated with the global pull of the sport.

In a few days I would be in Tete, where I could rest up and replenish before starting on the second part of the trip. I was already thinking about the food I would have, as the diet I had been on was really losing its appeal. The food I ate at the roadside was either dodgy-looking or bland and even the pasta and dried soup I was carrying had become dull. As a former paratrooper, I was happy to survive on limited and poor rations when I needed to, but I appreciated a good meal all the same.

Thirsty and needing a break, I stopped for some refreshment in a small place and chatted with two locals, despite our difficulty in understanding each other. Football crept up in the conversation and they were interested in talking about the English Premiership, clearly envied across the world.

Leaving the shop, the scenery began to change again with a twisting road surrounded by prominent hills. The bush was baked to a crisp and the only greenery was provided by scattered evergreen bushes. Occasionally, a cyclist on a clapped-out machine would ride by and look at me seriously as if I was in the wrong place, but I would smile at them, shouting out a greeting and they would ride on, a startled look on their faces.

I crossed over the Mpimbi River that flows into the Zambezi and considered looking for water, but the banks were almost vertical and I had to walk on. Stopping in Xeline towards the end of the day, I searched around for some hot food, but found only cold kapenta, which had no doubt been sitting out in the sun all day. Opting instead for a cold drink to clear the dust from my throat, I left and walked away, looking for a place to camp.

After a few kilometres, passing through small mud hut settlements where women were pounding cassava in oversized wooden mortars, some interesting looking rock formations appeared on my right, greying in the disappearing light. Leaving the road and heading for them, I found a sheltered spot out of view and began to collect firewood and brush. Quickly setting up camp, I made myself some pasta and settled down to enjoy the setting. The volcanic rock I was sitting on was still warm from the heat of the sun. Suitably fed and relaxed after a tough day, I curled into my tent and was soon asleep.

Despite the glorious setting, I had an uncomfortable night as the ground was rock hard and the temperature dipped in the early hours. I knew that several kilometres to the west of where I slept, David Livingstone had met his nemesis, the Cahora Bassa rapids (taken from the native word 'Kaorabasa' meaning 'finish', which presumably relates to the end of navigable water). One of the aims of his Zambezi expedition was to prove a route from the coast into central Africa, which he would dub 'God's Highway', to develop trade and the spread of Christianity in the region. A few days out of Tete, they hit the first of the rapids and passed through safely, but when the river narrowed to just twenty metres, a rock punctured one of their boats and they had to abandon the attempt. They tried several more times, including when the river was in flood, hoping that a steamer could pass over the rocks, but each time they failed, and the desired for river route into Central Africa was no more. Livingstone summed up his mood in his journal:

'Things look dark for our enterprise. This Kebrabasa is what I never expected. No hint of its nature ever reached my ears. The only person who ever saw the river was Jose St. Anna (a Portuguese trader), and he describes it as fearful when in flood. A Governor sent down two negroes in a canoe and neither they nor canoe was ever seen again'. (2)

Today, the Cahora Bassa Dam, completed by the Portuguese in 1974, stands further west upriver in the gorges, watching over the area where Livingstone was so valiantly defeated.

Packing up my gear, I was away early and strode out into the welcoming dawn. The road had begun to flatten out and the ups and downs had come to an end. Stopping for a mid-morning break, I bought a fruit drink and some biscuits from a shop and rested on a patio overlooking the road. Locals walked or cycled past, many throwing me a surprised glance.

Soon afterwards, a young man who was shoeless and dressed in dirty rags came to stand in front of me about ten feet away, a vacant expression on his face. He just looked at me with his arms by his side, not moving his head or body and not showing any emotion. It had happened once before in a village along the way and I reasoned that it was my skin colour and sudden appearance that had brought them to me. They were vagabonds, possibly thrown out of their communities and down on their luck and they seemed to spend their days wandering along tracks and roads waiting for something to happen. I termed them the 'Lost Ones' and would meet more of them on the road in the coming weeks.

Further on, I passed another timber yard with logs neatly stacked in rows. I was looking at thousands of years of steady growth, cut down in the blink of an eye. Someone was clearly making a lot of money from the trade and I doubted it was the villagers whose scorched land I had passed through. There were lorries coming in one end to drop off their load, whilst other even bigger vehicles were leaving for the coast with their colossal cargo.

After a few more hours, when I was thinking of a rest break, an off-roader pulled over and stopped in front of me. Walking over to the driver's side, I was pleasantly surprised to see Calvin and his wife, whose lodge I had stayed in just after arriving in country. They were on their way back from Tete to Zumbo and it was a stroke of luck that our paths had crossed. They were amazed that I had covered such a distance and encouraged me on to Tete, which was still over fifty kilometres away. Whilst we were chatting, Calvin gave me some contacts of people who could help me when I reached town. The expat network was alive again and I was glad for the support.

Later, after walking past some pretty villages set back from the road, their neat huts surrounded by impressive bare rock formations, I hit the outskirts of Tracado and sought out a bar. After several hours in the baking sun, I felt I had earnt some refreshment and time to relax in the shade. A policeman, sitting on the patio of the station, called out to me in Portuguese and I waved back but kept walking. I was fed up being stopped by officials and pseudo officials for no reason and a wave and continuing on usually did the trick. The officer, not put off, jogged up to me and began asking questions which I shrugged at and kept going. I told him that I had come from Zumbo and was walking to Tete, which brought a shocked look to his face. It was at this time that I noticed the gun on his hip and made sure that I kept smiling during our conversation.

We passed a large school with manicured lawns, the children dressed neatly in crisp blue and white matching uniforms. It was a far cry from what I had experienced around Lake Cahora Bassa, where I had seen little evidence of school buildings at all and where kids frolicked in the dirt, often dressed in rags. Bushes with resplendent lilac and yellow flowers lined one of the walls, in stark contrast to the surrounding desiccated bush.

Even the shops looked smart, displaying their wares out front, the ground around them freshly swept and clean. In between the questioning, I asked the policeman where I could find a bar and he took me to a place on the far edge of town. On entering, I saw a female colleague of his, with stripes down her arm, drinking a beer in the corner and so joined her. It was good there was electricity in the town and the cold liquid felt wonderful as it disappeared rapidly down my throat.

The policeman continued firing questions at me. Finally realising that I wasn't able to understand him, he then asked to see my passport which I handed over. Slowly flicking through the pages and studying my visa, he soon lost interest and with a chuckle began chatting with his friend. Once I was refreshed and ready to continue, I looked around the stalls for something to eat, but there was nothing that appealed, only stinking fish and parts of a goat, so I walked back to the road.

Outside of town, I crossed over a long modern bridge over the river Mavuzi with only small pools of water below glinting in the sun and began to climb a long and steep section, winding through the hills. Half way up, a car pulled over and a European-looking man walked over and began speaking to me in Spanish interspersed with a few English words. It sounded like he had seen me before and was interested in my trip and keen to help. Reaching into his car, he handed me a bunch of bananas which I thanked him for, before continuing. The bananas were quite small with greenish skin, but were a real boost and I enjoyed them as I suffered up the climb.

A few hours later, I stopped at a makeshift drinks stand by the side of the road for a quick rest. A man with olive brown skin and Mediterranean looks wandered over and began questioning me about my journey.

'I've never heard of people walking the Zambezi!' he said.

'Yes, a few have done it,' I replied, 'albeit in stages. David Livingstone is the most famous, but he never made it to the source.'

'Ah, Mr Livingstone. A very famous man!'

'Do you know much about him?' I asked, interested to learn the reach of his reputation.

'Of course. The children here learn about him in school and he is well respected.'

Interested to hear more about my trip, he invited me to rest in his house with his wife, located just behind the shop. Taking off my pack, I relaxed on the sofa while sipping cold cola and watching the BBC news. Mozambique was a funny place so far, I thought. One minute you would be toiling in the sun and the next you would be relaxing in someone's house, enjoying their hospitality.

My host was called 'Charles' and he was originally from Portugal, but had worked in South Africa, where he had learnt to speak English. After several years there, he had decided to settle in Mozambique with his wife, as they both enjoyed the climate and simple way of life. He supplied chickens to the surrounding restaurants and towns and seemed to be doing well, judging by the size and décor of his home.

We talked about my route so far and he gave me some

useful advice on which way to go. He also told me to ask for the *Mfumu*, village leader, whenever I needed somewhere to sleep and this knowledge helped me a great deal in the weeks to come. It was the first time I had heard the word and he explained that the Mfumu, elected by the community, had a responsibility for the wellbeing of people travelling through their area.

After I had rested and as I was leaving, he presented me with a bottle of mineral water, a large bottle of ice and some tins of food. I accepted gratefully, but staggered down the road with a pack four kilos heavier than it had been an hour before. The bottle of ice was particularly appreciated, because as it melted I could take a cooling drink, which made a change from the tepid water I had in my bottle.

The break had been excellent, but it had cost me time and as the light began to fade, I searched around for somewhere to stay. I came to a village spread out along the road and saw a 'snake patrol' coming the other way, consisting of two teenage boys with sticks and a dog out in front. I had heard of these patrols from one of the rangers on Lake Cahora Bassa, who had told me that every village had them. At dusk and dawn teenagers, sometimes with a dog, would be sent out to circle the settlement a few times and look for snakes, which were attracted there by mice and rats. They were taught from an early age to have a healthy respect for serpents, treat them with caution and would kill any they found.

Further on, I asked for the Mfumu and was directed to an older man lounging on a chair. Explaining that I was on the way to Tete, I dropped my head to the side and placed my hand against it, indicating that I wanted to sleep in the village. My display had worked a few times before, but the man just laughed, shook his head and waved me away. Taking the hint and feeling a little dejected, I left the village and set out again into the gathering darkness.

I stopped a few more times at individual homes to ask if I could put up my tent, but despite my smiles was waved away as if I was an unwelcome vagrant. As I continued on, there were no lights marking the road and few vehicles going past, but every so often I would see cooking fires burning to the left and right of me, as the women prepared dinner outside their huts.

Choosing to walk in the middle of the thoroughfare to avoid the brush alongside it, I would occasionally put my head torch on to check there were no snakes in my path. I knew that they sometimes curled up for warmth on the tarmac that was baked by the sun during the day, and didn't want any surprises. Sometimes I would get a fright when my shoe brushed against something, or I spotted an object in front of me, but invariably it turned out to be rubber from part of a tyre or a piece of old clothing. When travelling along roads in Zambia, we had often seen dead snakes on the tarmac, some of them sizeable, flattened by vehicles but still formidable-looking even in death.

As it was fully dark now, I knew it would probably be hopeless trying to seek permission to camp in a village and anyway, I didn't want to give anyone a fright as a mzungu appearing out of the gloom! Even though I was tired, I was actually enjoying my walk in the dark. It was still warm, although cooling and I was making steady progress on the hard surface. I continued to look for possible campsites by the side of the road, but nothing appealed.

Eventually, as it passed 8pm, I knew I had to find a spot and began to scan the terrain more earnestly. I had been on the go more than thirteen hours and needed to rest. Taking out my torch, I found some waste ground set back from the road and walked into it. Looking around, I saw the faint glimmer of a fire in the distance, but calculated that I was far enough away not to be seen.

Working quickly, I put up my tent, got out my sleeping gear and prepared for bed. As I was closing my pack, my torch caught the eyes of something in the grass close by and, a little spooked, I walked over to see what it was. A brown spider, about two inches across, stared back at me without moving, its eyes reflecting the light. I hoped that I wouldn't see it again in the night.

Wandering back to my tent, I was just about to step inside, when I heard a shout. Peering hard into the darkness and keeping dead still, I could just make out the glimmer of another fire in the distance that I hadn't spotted earlier.

A few moments passed and I thought the incident was over, but there was another shout, this time louder. Crouching by my tent for about ten minutes and keeping dead still, I hoped that I wasn't the cause of the anxiety. I then picked up the sound of footsteps in the still night, as figures moved through the brush. Long before they got close to me, I put on my torch and shouted out 'Tourist! Tourist!' trying to explain who I was. Slowly, some men moved into the torchlight from the direction of the road and I saw movement from the scrub behind me.

'Tourist! Tourist!!' I called out again, followed by 'Ingles, Ingles' the word for an English person in Portuguese.

The new arrivals formed a semicircle around me, my tent at my back, and I noticed they were all carrying weapons of various kinds, from wooden clubs to rocks to slingshots. The men, about twelve of them, were all dressed in old trousers and shirts and their stern and questioning faces glared back at me. To show I wasn't a threat, I removed my headtorch and directed the light into my face, so that they could see who I was. I hadn't had a shave for a few days and knew that my face was probably dirty, but felt that seeing my white skin would persuade them that I was a traveller just passing through.

After what seemed an age, one of the older men spoke up and began to ask me questions, pointing his finger accusingly in my direction. I couldn't understand what he was asking, but continued to let them know that I was a tourist and English. I also pointed to my tent, indicating that I was tired and wanted to sleep there.

This went on for some time, with others in the group throwing questions in my direction and pointing at me. To try to placate my audience, I told them about the places I had visited, including Zumbo, Fingoe and Xeline and that I was heading for Tete. The mention of the town, the largest in the province, seemed to strike a chord as they began to understand that I was heading there. Some of the men spoke to each other and I wondered if they were talking about moving me on, or something more sinister.

As they were talking, I spotted the tins that Charles had given me a few hours earlier next to my pack and handed one of them to my questioner. He took the baked beans from me, studying the tin thoroughly and grinned, and for the first time the mood seemed to lift. I told him that they were good to eat by rubbing my stomach and giving the thumbs up and he agreed, smiling broadly.

A few moments later, I heard the strangest of sounds. There were thuds on the ground, as the men with rocks dropped them behind their backs and out of sight, having realised that I was not a threat.

I asked if I could stay by pointing at the tent again and laying my head in my hand and the man turned to his friends and discussed it for a few moments. Some voices seemed angry, but the majority were calm and I saw a few nodding heads as consensus was reached. The man turned to me, pointed at the tent and nodded, indicating that I could stay there. He also said a few words, which I assumed were about me moving on the next day, but I had no intention of overstaying my welcome. Shaking his hand, I thanked him as the rest of the figures moved slowly away, back into the darkness.

Watching them go, I breathed out hard and thought about what could have happened. They were probably worried about thieves or bandits trying to steal from them; I would hear about this later. The fact they were all armed showed that they were ready for a fight and I was glad that the situation hadn't turned ugly. Clambering into my tent, I settled down to write up my diary, glad that the crisis had passed and I hadn't been told to pack up and find somewhere else to sleep.

Later on, I heard muffled voices outside and, unzipping the tent, found an old man in a tattered suit standing there with his wife. He pointed to himself, smiling, and said, 'Mfumu, Mfumu.' Shaking his hand, I told him that I understood and that I appreciated being allowed to stay. I was pleased that the couple appeared to be in good spirits and happy for me to be there. The man kept reaching over to me and shaking my hand, as if I was some long-lost friend and I expected him to ask for money at any minute, but he just continued to look at me. After a few more minutes of hand shaking and hearing where I had come from, he led his wife away.

Twenty minutes later, as my eyelids were getting heavy and I was settling down to sleep, I heard more voices approaching. Unzipping my tent once again, I stepped outside to find about twenty locals, men and women, looking shyly at me in the torchlight. A man stepped forward, telling me in English that he was from Malawi and that the people had come to see what the fuss was all about. They had heard that a strange man in a funny house had arrived in the village and they wanted to have a look. I suppose it was strange in their eyes, probably like a spaceship landing on an English village green.

He asked what I was doing there and I went through my story again, explaining that I was off to Tete the following day. He translated to the rest of the group and I could see the surprised and amused expressions on the faces of his companions. Explaining that it was too far to walk, he said I should take a car instead, but he didn't understand the ethos of the expedition. In much of Mozambique people walk everywhere because there are few cars, but they walk out of necessity and not on expeditions or for leisure.

After a few minutes of conversation, the man told me that I should come to his house to rest because he was worried about me, but didn't elaborate. As I was already established and didn't want to be a burden, I thanked him and told him that I was happy where I was and wanted to stay there. Soon afterwards, the group left and I could hear them chattering to each other as they made their way home.

The following morning, as I was packing up my tent, a large group of villagers wandered over. They seemed interested in where I had slept and chuckled to each other as if seeing something for the first time. In the daylight, I saw the huts clearly, a few hundred metres away partially hidden by trees and it was no wonder I hadn't spotted them in the dark. I waved goodbye to my new friends and walked back to the road, still quiet in the first blooms of morning.

It was about twenty kilometres to Tete, which I knew I could cover in four to five hours, so it was going to be an easy day. When I had phone reception I called Rudi, one of the contacts given to me by Calvin the day before. He said he was happy to put me up for a few days and I was looking forward to some decent rest in the provincial capital.

Climbing a hill a few hours into the trek, I saw a pile of large rocks by the side of the road and next to it, a man was smashing one into smaller pieces. Scattered around him were piles of smaller rocks of various sizes that were the result of his efforts and to one side were bags of stones for sale. I watched him for a few moments as he wielded his mallet, stone shards flying everywhere, and wondered what the smaller stones were used for, amazed that he could make a living from such hard work. As I got closer to Tete, I would see more of these workers, sometimes women, toiling in the heat, more bags of stones next to them for sale and deduced that they were used in the construction industry in some way.

It was close to this point on the opposite side of the Zambezi that the veteran adventurer David Lemon collapsed with cerebral malaria. The mosquitoes of Cahora Bassa had finally broken through his defences and he had to suspend his walk and seek treatment in neighbouring South Africa. After treatment and recuperation, he returned to Tete a month later to resume his trek.

The country had fully flattened out by now and there

wasn't a hill to be seen. I passed fields full of yellowing wheat lining the road, one of the few signs of large-scale agriculture I had seen in the country. There were storage silos to hold the grain and everything looked organised and neat. Closer to town were industrial units and truck depots, with workers in oily dungarees walking around with purpose, tools clanging noisily in the air.

A little further on, a tuk-tuk went past me and pulled over to the side in flurry of dust. Reaching it, I saw that the passenger in the back was a local woman dressed in smart, flowing clothes who asked if I wanted a lift into town. She told me that it was too hot to walk and although I agreed with her, I declined her invitation, telling her I was walking to the sea.

'No, you must come!' she insisted, making room on the seat.

I told her again that I had to remain on foot and she told me that she had just returned from church and felt it her duty to help. Smiling and thanking her again, I told her that stopping was kindness in itself and that I had to decline her offer. Giving me one of the widest smiles I had seen, she waved, wished me good luck and ordered the driver to carry on.

Chapter Six - Tete

The outskirts of Tete began to build several kilometres out. The lorry depots and heavy machinery outlets were gradually replaced by a shanty town, where homes were made from corrugated iron, plastic sheets and rough logs. As I progressed, the homes gradually improved, many being made of brick, stone and glass, with some even having electric cables leading into the roof. Getting closer to the centre still, the dwellings smartened up further, surrounded with fences and gardens out front. The level of traffic was also starting to build and I had to take care as the cars and motorbikes had strange ideas about sharing the road.

I hit a bustling T-junction; the road on the left led to Malawi and to the right a few kilometres away, the bridge over the mighty Zambezi River. Small minibuses dropping off and collecting passengers plagued the junction and I was glad to be heading towards the river. The next few kilometres to the bridge felt overwhelming: there were so many people, it was a shock to the senses. After the tranquillity of the previous weeks, I even found it a little depressing. Tuk-tuks and taxis, something I hadn't seen in the countryside of course, honked their horns and weaved from side to side on the road to get the attention of potential passengers.

Calling Rudi as I walked past the busy shops and throngs of people, we agreed to meet at the bridge. I stopped for a cold drink at a small restaurant and was dismayed when the waiter tried to shortchange me, probably seeing me as an easy target. I wondered what would happen if he tried it on with the locals.

I saw the bridge a few minutes later with its tall white arches and was elated and relieved that I had made the halfway point on my journey. It had taken me nineteen days, including a few rest days, to cover the five hundred kilometres from Zumbo and I was pleased with my progress. As people swirled around me, I was fixated with the bridge, a sight I had longed for on the dusty days to reach it. The Samora Machel Bridge was impressive, finished in 1973 and named after the president at the time; it is one of only three road bridges in the country that crosses the Zambezi.

Tete was already an important Swahili trading centre, established on the southern shore but today straddling both banks, before the arrival of the Portuguese in 1531. The Europeans were drawn to Mozambique by stories of gold in the surrounding hills. Under their rule, the town prospered with Portuguese families settling there and it became a hub in the flow of ivory and slaves down to the coast. Thereafter, when coal and other minerals were found in the province, it continued to prosper, attracting nationals in the search for work. When Mozambique gained its independence from Portugal in 1974, there was an exodus of the ethnic Portuguese and much of the expertise and investment left town with them.

Sitting in the shade by a shack selling dried fish, I looked around me trying to take in the hustle, bustle and development. Rudi picked me up shortly afterwards and welcomed me with a strong handshake, as if he had known me for years. He was of medium height with a big chest and thick arms, his tanned face giving away his love of being outdoors. An easy-going manner and quick wit made him a great companion and it was good to talk about the world in irreverent terms, something I had missed on the road.

After throwing my pack onto the seats, we drove back to his home which was on the north bank in one of the more affluent areas. The house he rented was a single-storey, whitewashed and neat affair surrounded by high walls, jagged razor wire glinting in the sunshine. Seeing me eying the protection, he gave me a knowing smile and waggled his finger.

'Can't be too careful!' he warned in his South African drawl.

'Is it dangerous around here?' I asked.

'Sometimes. We had a local climb the wall a few months

ago and get into the garden, but he regretted it when the dog put him in hospital!'

The Samora Machel Bridge at Tete,
the halfway point on my journey

'Nasty!' I winced.

'Yeah, the bugger was trying his luck, probably seeing if he could steal something. He even wanted me to pay his medical bills!'

The dog that had attacked the man, a young thick-set Rottweiler, growled at me as I walked across the yard and Rudi delivered a swift reprimand, telling the beast that I was a guest. Thereafter, the dog and I became friends, particularly when I threw him a ball around the yard. There were two other canines about, but they were older and smaller and were more useful as an early warning system in case of intruders.

After a much-needed shower, I joined Rudi for lunch, couscous with lamb which was wonderful and filling, and my host began to tell me about his life in Mozambique. He had come from South Africa a few years before, after his country had taken a turn for the worse and had made it difficult for white people to progress. He called it 'white genocide' and hearing his stories, I could understand why. White farmers were being driven off their land and in some cases murdered; the best jobs in government and the private sector were reserved for those with black skin. It seemed almost like reverse apartheid and it was easy to see why Rudi and many of his contemporaries had left the country to seek opportunities elsewhere.

Rudi lived with his wife Laura, who worked in a building supplies depot in town. She had originally come from Zimbabwe, but left after problems in that country too. Rudi was an entrepreneur, involved in selling engines and vehicle parts and was in the process of setting up a fuel business in Zumbo. There was currently no petrol station in the town and vehicles had to drive hours to fill up their tanks, so it looked like an interesting proposition.

As we chatted on the porch about life in Mozambique, it was great to fully relax and not worry about covering a certain distance or looking for somewhere to sleep. It was great also to walk to the fridge and pour a glass of cold apple juice or chomp on a piece of European cheese, delicacies that I hadn't had since entering the country and was unlikely to see again for the rest of the journey.

When Laura returned later in the day, we chatted over dinner with a glass of wine and I marveled at the life they had established, despite the difficulties. It seemed the Mozambicans made that life quite difficult for the expats, with their bureaucracy and red tape, but the community stuck with it and got on with living. My hosts were fascinated with my journey, incredulous that I would take on such a challenge, and promised to help me prepare for the next phase.

The couple kindly put me up in a chalet next to the house and it felt wonderful to ease my aching body in between the clean sheets and feel at home. Their Wi-Fi allowed me to send messages to loved ones about my progress and to check up on world headlines to see what I had been missing. As I was trying to drift off to sleep, a mosquito buzzed by my ear followed by another and another and I was reminded how close to the river I was, and forced under the covers for sanctuary for the rest of the night.

The following day after breakfast, Rudi and I sat down to discuss what I needed to do to continue my journey. He had kindly agreed to take the day off and drive me around town to help out. I basically had three priorities: visa extension, money and food in that order. The second one was easily accomplished while the third, which needed a little more time, we saved for later.

The visa extension was a different matter, with Rudi telling me that the immigration officials loved their procedures and it could take much of the day to sort out. The visa I had been issued with in Lusaka was for one month, of which I had already used up a few weeks, and it wasn't going to last me as far as the ocean. I needed to extend it and we set off into town to plead my case.

Driving over the bridge into the southern part of town, Rudi turned to me with a serious look on his face.

'They found a body on the riverbank a week ago,' he said, pointing to a spot. 'They reckon a local was taken by a crocodile further upstream and he ended up here.'

'Seriously? Quite a shock for the people here to see the body, I would imagine?'

'Not really, they see it all the time. Fishermen and women washing their clothes by the river get attacked by crocodiles on a regular basis and it's just one of those things. They can be huge as well; one was caught a year back that was nearly fifteen feet long! Be careful when you're close to the river, as these buggers can creep up on you in shallow water and grab you before you know it!'

'Good advice!' I replied, as I glanced uneasily down at the murky water.

We entered the older part of town where the government offices and law courts were located and headed with trepidation for immigration, as the heat began to build. Rudi could speak some Portuguese, so he asked an official what I needed to do to extend the visa. The man told him that I simply needed to provide a letter informing the authorities of my arrival in Tete. In a quiet corner, Rudi told me that they changed the rules all the time and that the letter was probably a red herring. We returned to the official, informing him that we would provide a letter and he told us that I now also had to see the 'Director'.

'They make it up as they go along,' Rudi murmured under his breath as we walked along the corridor.

'Seems a bit excessive to have to see the head man when all I want is an extension,' I replied.

'Welcome to Mozambique!' he whispered with a grin.

Waiting in an anteroom for the Head of Immigration to see us was an experience. Groups of officials and individuals of varying ranks would come and go from his office with papers and documents and then scurry off to carry out his wishes. After an hour, we were led in to see him to discuss my request. He was aged about forty with tinges of grey in his short cut frizzy hair and his dark uniform resonated with authority. Rudi explained my request to him carefully and he nodded slowly in understanding as he occasionally glanced at me. At length, the man agreed to the extension, and stated that he wanted a letter from me requesting it. The 'arrival letter' was apparently no longer required. He also told Rudi that he would have to stand surety for my time in country and have to provide details of his work permit and other documents.

Thanking the man, we left the building feeling we had made some progress and drove the fifteen minutes over to Laura's office to write the letter and get copies of the documents required. We then returned to immigration, back over the Zambezi, to see the Director again, but were informed he had gone out and that we should return later.

'Is it always like this?' I asked Rudi in frustration, as we strolled back to the car.

'Pretty much, although it's easier to extend when you have a work permit and residency. As you're just passing through, it seems a little more complicated. I think they like to keep tabs on visitors.'

We found a bustling Lebanese restaurant nearby and consoled ourselves with chicken kebabs and cold drinks, before returning to see the Director. He was back, but we had to wait another hour to see him. He wasn't happy with the letter, as it was written from me and in English. He told us that it had to come from Rudi and not from me. It would have been helpful if we had been told this earlier, but we gritted our teeth, found a quiet area and began to compose the letter, with Rudi checking the translation app on his phone to make sure we were writing sense.

Checking the letter with one of the officials at the desk, we were then told that I had to complete a series of forms (in Portuguese) to accompany the letter. This was also a new requirement that the Director hadn't told us about. The forms, apart from asking for the normal personal data that you would expect, also wanted work history, qualifications and a range of other topics that seemed unusual for a visa extension.

We completed the forms, paid the fee and began to think we were getting somewhere until the official told us to return in a week to collect it. I was hoping to start my trek again the following day and the thought of having to return to Tete when I was half way to the ocean horrified me, knowing how difficult it would be to get back.

After more discussion, pleading and biting of tongues, the visa was finally handed over after we told the man that the Director had promised it would be issued that day. As Rudi and I walked back to the car, we chuckled. We felt the white lie was justified, after all we had been through. From arriving at the immigration office in the morning to receiving the visa extension in my hand, it had taken over five hours.

We crossed back over the bridge and pulled into a depot selling oil and lubricants, Rudi telling me I should meet a friend of his inside. Donald was one of the managers of the place and had boated along much of the river in Mozambique. He was a great source of information on what I could expect in the coming weeks. We pored over maps and satellite photos, discussing in detail the river and its characteristics as it meandered its way to the ocean.

'So, should I take the north or south bank?' I asked him towards the end of our discussion.

'Difficult to say,' he replied, giving me a steady frown. 'There are tracks relatively close to the river for most of the way down, but there's a nasty hilly section on the north side after a few days of travel. You could be wandering around there for days, trying to find a way through. It's bad on the south side too, but I think there are tracks over the hills.'

'Looks like the south side then!' I grinned, studying the map again.

'Yeah, probably a good choice. There's a route pretty much all the way down to Caia, which is about three hundred kilometres down. If you stay on the southern side from there, you'll run into marshes lower down, so you could cross the bridge at that point and stay on the north bank all the way to Chinde. The going is firmer there but the mosquitoes are horrendous! You'll have to get a boat for the last section of course, back across the Zambezi, as your end point is on an island.'

I knew that David Lemon had taken a similar route a few years earlier. I asked Donald what routes were available beyond Caia and he knew of some tracks by the river, but wasn't sure about the whole section. Thanking him for his advice, with routes and terrain swirling around my head, I decided to have another look at my satnav later in the day before making a final decision on which way to go.

Next, Rudi and I drove to 'Shoprite', the main

supermarket in Tete and close to his home. It was a large place, with room for hundreds of cars and a Kentucky Fried Chicken (KFC) restaurant adjacent. In the whole time I had been in Mozambique, I hadn't seen anything like it and wouldn't for the rest of the journey. Where before I had seen shops with the bare essentials, this place was like heaven, with rows and rows of food piled high to the rafters; fruits of every kind, cheese, sliced meats, delicacies and drink. The locals I saw in the store, dressed in smart clothes, were obviously well-to-do with money to spend. There were also quite a few white and Far Eastern looking people browsing the aisles and I wondered where they would have shopped before Shoprite was built. All I needed was some pasta, dried soups and nuts, as it would be difficult to find them once I had left Tete. My trusty diet would be supplemented by biscuits, fruit, chicken and fish that I would find along the way.

Returning to the house, we had some tea to celebrate our achievements of the day and got ready for the evening, as the three of us were going out for some entertainment. 'Anna Marie's Place', with pool and bar, was on the edge of town, tucked away behind warehouses and an oasis for the thirsty expat. Beer-branded fridges, a long wooden bar and friendly staff were worth trekking five hundred kilometres for. South Africans were the main customers and it was good to relax in a comfortable, safe place and enjoy some decent food.

Before long, the karaoke had started up and after listening to the competition, Rudi and I had a go with our own renditions, including 'Whole Lotta Rosie' by AC/DC which was fun for us, but perhaps not for the audience. It was great to have some social activity after living rough for weeks, and the memories of the evening would stay in my mind all the way to Chinde. We got home late and after bidding my hosts goodnight, I settled down to rest. Earlier, I had been given an anti-mosquito plug, which had dispersed the pesky insects and as I thought through the routes again in my head, I drifted off in peaceful sleep.

The following morning, after a relaxed breakfast, Rudi drove me down to the bridge for me to continue my trek. As we passed locals walking along the road, going about their business, I reflected on the town of Tete. It was a boom town in every sense, with its population doubling to three hundred thousand in just a decade, with evidence of rapid expansion everywhere. Despite there being some smart houses, most required their own water pumps, and septic tanks were the norm as there was no networked sewage system.

My host had told me about the rising crime in the town, which forced homeowners to protect their properties like fortresses. Electric gates, barbed wire and floodlights were commonplace for homes in some suburbs, where selected dwellings had been hit several times. The town was crowded and dirty, with rubbish everywhere and stray dogs patrolled the neighbourhoods looking for their next meal.

When David Livingstone visited Tete, he described it as standing on a succession of low sandstone ridges on the right (south) bank of the Zambezi; a wall of stone and mud surrounded the village and the native population lived in huts outside. It was a major centre for the slave and ivory trade. Gold and coal were evident in the area, but were not actively mined due to the importance of the other trades.

I was grateful for my stay, which had allowed me to rest and re-engage with my own world, but I was glad to be leaving the dirt and squalor and looking forward to hitting the trail again. Walking over the bridge, having decided to trek on the southern bank, I glanced to my left and saw a concrete embankment with a steel crane rusting away. It had obviously once been used to unload goods from passing boats, but was now on the way to falling in the river. It seemed sad that infrastructure, designed to improve people's lives and the efficiency of the town, was allowed to decay in such a way.

Looking down at the river, I wondered how much of it I would see in the coming weeks. The water was a muddy brown colour and logs and uprooted bushes floated gently by. At this point the river was about eight hundred metres across, but I knew that lower down, it would spread out and be as much as thee kilometres wide. As I walked, minibuses and cars raced past me, tootling their horns, with passengers staring at me as if I were from a different planet.

Reaching the far bank, I turned left and strolled past simple shops and houses before emerging, half an hour later, on the edge of town. I called home, whilst I still had a signal and relayed events of the expedition, before striding out again, looking for a path to the river.

Chapter Seven - Back into the Wild

I found a track that looked promising and followed it for a while before it hit some small farms and I had to jump fences and cross waste ground to get around them. I picked up another path that led me over low hills, before it dropped me into a shanty town, the homes made of rough wood and plastic sheets. The locals, surprised at my appearance, were friendly enough and smiled when I called out a 'bom dia' greeting. Some of the younger children ran away behind huts, whilst the teenagers grinned at me as music blared in the background. I was reminded of David Livingstone's own observations when travelling along the Zambezi:

'If we met a child, the moment he raised his eyes he would take to his heels in an agony of terror, such as we might feel if we met a live Egyptian mummy at the door of the British museum. Alarmed by the child's wild outcries, the mother rushes out of her hut, but darts back again at the first glimpse of the same fearful apparition.' (1)

The track eventually hit a tarmac road that crossed over a new bridge, built to take trucks away from the old bridge and Tete itself. The Kassuende Bridge gently arching over the river and completed in 2014, was a wonderful sight, its pale concrete sections shining like beacons and untarnished by time. It was a sign of progress for the country, something that I felt was desperately needed and hadn't seen much evidence of on my journey. I walked up to the start of the structure and looked eastwards, hoping to see a path following the river, but observed only marshland, glinting with water in the morning sunshine. Retracing my steps and consulting my Sygic device, I located a track back from the river that looked suitable and headed for it, weaving my way around farm huts.

Eventually, it joined another path that took me close to the water. The well-worn route was on a bank about ten foot above the marsh and twisted and turned through bushes, occasionally giving me glimpses of the river.

After an hour I bumped into a man, possibly a farmer, coming the other way.

'Is this route good?' I asked him, giving a thumbs up and pointing along the path.

'Nao,' he said, shaking his head and pointing insistently to the south.

'Eh? It looks fine,' I uttered, peering into the distance.

'Terminar,' the man said, running an index finger rapidly across his throat in an alarming way but I figured he meant it was the track that terminated.

'Obrigado,' I replied, thanking him. 'I'll just have a look and take it from there.'

The man shrugged, gave me a half-hearted wave and sauntered away. I couldn't believe the path would just end when it looked so well established, so continued on, knowing that I would have to deal with whatever arose. After a few more kilometres, the path indeed began to narrow and as I turned a corner it stopped altogether. I tried to see a way forward across the boggy ground but there was none, only high grasses with no evidence of a way through.

Frustrated, I let out a deep sigh and sat on my pack to take a drink, plotting my next move. I was hoping to find a path that would take me all the way to the sea, but in the coming days would be constantly thwarted by unreliable routes that twisted and turned away from the river. Picking myself up, I walked the way I had come for some distance and then pushed through head-high vegetation, until finally emerging on the edge of some cultivation.

Picking my way carefully through the farmland, taking care to avoid the crops, I scanned the ground in front, hoping to find a better path. Skirting the edges of fields and climbing a series of mud banks, I eventually found another track that looked promising, parallel with the river, and took it, hoping for better luck.

I passed through a few small settlements with homes made of mud and sticks, and later stopped at a small brick building that sold drinks. Taking off my pack I sat in the shade, enjoying a moment of respite from the searing sun. Small motorbikes passed noisily by, loaded down with beer crates and boxes, plying their trade along the river.

A couple of men joined me under the flimsy roof and asked where I was going. I told them I was heading for Chinde on the Indian Ocean and simulated a swimming motion, to which they chuckled and shook their heads in amusement. They had obviously heard of the place, judging by their reaction, but I imagined had never been; they just knew it was a long way away and probably thought me quite mad.

I had calculated that it was just over four hundred kilometres away and estimated that it would take about two weeks to reach, depending on the terrain and difficulty of route. I was still in good shape and fit from walking across half of Mozambique and didn't have any injuries, so was confident about making it to the sea in reasonable time.

Suitably refreshed, I headed back into the heat, glad of the presence of the river in the distance. The rutted track, wide enough for a car at this point, wound its way eastwards, but when it came to flat, open ground would sometimes disappear in different directions, with the routes unclear to an outsider. I would follow one path, but invariably have to choose another when it curled away in the wrong direction. Sygic, my simple satnav, showed few of the routes by the river and I ended up having to navigate through compass bearings, guesswork and gut instinct.

Once back on track and close to the river, I made good progress on the level ground and apart from the odd motorbike that fizzed by, was completely on my own. In the middle of the afternoon, I came to a magical section with trees either side of the path, providing much needed shade. To my left, the Zambezi flowed gently by, keeping pace with me. It lasted for a few kilometres and then the magic disappeared as the path turned inland over some hills and I lost sight of the river.

A few hours from dusk, when the track came close to the

river again, I began to look for somewhere to camp. The ideal was to find a clearing by the water, but the vegetation was too thick. Eventually, I came to a spot on a secondary level above the river, away from the track and heaved off my pack with relief. It had been a long and sweaty day after the stopover in Tete and although I had only covered about twenty kilometres, the winding route and dead ends had frustrated me and I had pushed myself hard and needed to rest.

Taking a moment to enjoy the setting, I watched as swallows, lapwing, bee-eaters and swifts danced in the air, some swooping down to the water before rising up and landing on branches nearby. I was pleased there were no mosquitoes to spoil my vigil, but expected them to arrive at any moment.

After I had erected my tent, I noticed dried hippo dung off to one side and thought about moving, but decided against it and walked down the bank for some water. The reeds had been forced aside by the huge herbivores and it looked like a favourite haul out point for them. I listened to see if they were close, but not hearing anything I pushed my bottle under the surface to collect what I needed.

I had lit a fire and put my titanium mug on it to boil some water when I heard the unmistakable sound of a motorbike puttering along the path and soon afterwards it came into view. Seeing my tent through the bushes, the figure rode his machine over to me and raised his hand in greeting when he stopped. Charles, who spoke a little English, was on his way home after visiting Tete and with a big smile on his face asked me what I was doing there. I thought he was going to tell me to move on, and when I asked him if it was alright to sleep there, he just shrugged his shoulders and didn't seem bothered. I think it was public land as it was well away from the path and miles from anywhere. Warming himself by the fire, he asked about my journey and the places I had seen.

The perfect camping spot on the banks of the Zambezi River

'You have come very far!' he told me, patting me on the back. 'Not even I have been to Zumbo or the lake and I have a bike.'

'You should go,' I answered. 'It's very different from here. There are mountains there, thick jungle and a lake the size of a sea!'

'Maybe, one day, if I have the time.'

It struck me that it would probably be expensive to travel so far by motorbike, when he was probably poor and perhaps viewed such a trip as too much of an indulgence. In the developed world, the opportunity to seek out new places and explore the country in which we live is something we often take for granted.

We chatted about his life in Mozambique and he seemed happy with his lot, having a wife, children and a home. He informed me that he had a shop a few hours away on my route and I promised to drop in the following day. I watched him chug away on his bike through the trees, as I tucked into my dinner of pasta and dry stir-in sauce and marveled at how lucky I was to undertake such an expedition.

I woke to a cool morning and the sound of hippos grunting

in the river and was glad they hadn't paid me a visit. They spend more time on land than many people realise and often stray far from the water at night, in search of the best grazing. Getting the fire going again, I made some coffee to the continual sounds of the hippos and gazed over the mist, slowly rising off the river. As I clutched my mug, I remembered that David Livingstone also enjoyed a warm beverage on mornings like this:

'Our greatest luxury in travelling was tea or coffee. We never once carried sugar enough to last a journey, but coffee is always good, while the sugarless tea is only bearable, because of the unbearable gnawing feeling of want and sinking which ensues if we begin to travel in the mornings without something warm in the stomach.' (1)

Packing up, I hit the twisty trail again in the cool of the morning and was pleased that it once again followed close to river. I spotted the tracks made by Charles's tyres and admired his riding skill when I noticed how close they were to the drop offs down to the water. After a few kilometres the path turned sharply inland, climbing through a small rocky gorge and then tracked parallel, although a long way from the river. I passed a herd of cows taking shade near some acacia trees, their white and brown coats looking somehow out of place in such a wild area. There was no sign of a guardian, which seemed strange with such valuable stock, but the herder was probably nearby, sleeping after a long night of protection.

A few hours later, I stopped at the shop owned by Charles and took a drink in the shade. It was a well-stocked establishment, with goods piled high to the roof, unlike many of the places I had visited where the shelves were often paltry or bare. Little children peeked at me from the corner of the building and then ran off excitedly, no doubt wondering who the strange visitor was. Those who ventured closer were rewarded with biscuits. In a land where there is so much poverty and danger, I wanted their experience of seeing a mzungu to be a good one.

I spoke to my host about the route ahead and he assured me that although there were rivers to cross and difficult, hilly sections to climb, there was a good path all the way to Sena, a few hundred kilometres away. I thanked him for his local knowledge and knew that I would rely on others for information as I progressed.

As I was leaving, an open topped truck pulled up and began to take on people and goods. Those who climbed over the rail began to settle themselves down and pulled scarves and shirts over their heads to shield from the sun. The truck would pass me an hour later, bouncing along the rocky track and despite the obvious discomfort, most of the faces I glimpsed were smiling.

Leaving the village, I passed a football field and saw through the brush a ragged set of hills in the distance. I was only about a kilometre from the Zambezi, but the bowl I was in was like an oven, without a breath of wind. My sweat quickly dried and I had to keep taking swigs of water in order to remain hydrated. Travelling at a similar time of year to me, David Lemon had also struggled with the heat:

'By ten in the morning the temperature would be up in the high thirties and by early afternoons, we all felt as though we were walking through a furnace.' (3)

After a few hours, the track curled sharply to the right and then stopped by some acacia trees at the base of a steep ridge. I could see the well-worn path up the rocky slope made by countless pairs of feet and slowly headed upwards. Twenty minutes later I made the summit and found a small group of locals catching their breath, chatting and laughing, traipsing across the rock. Following behind them, we soon dropped down the ridge and walked through a sparsely wooded area, before arriving at a small settlement. The huts, surrounded by thorny trees, overlooked the wide Luenha River that sparkled in the sunlight. It marked the boundary between the Tete and Manica provinces, although you wouldn't know it because the region hardly had any road signs, let alone boundary markers. It was the kind of idyllic spot that I had imagined when thinking about the expedition and I would have camped, but it was only early afternoon and I still had ground to cover.

The Luenha River flows into the Zambezi a few kilometres to the north and as it was the dry season, I could see people wading across it. It was a few hundred metres wide and flowed gently past without a care in the world. Taking off my shoes and rolling up my trousers, I followed the others in, surprised at how cold the water was. It was shallow, only flowing up to my knees in places, but it felt great on such a warm day and the sandy bottom helped to gently massage my feet. There was no danger of crocodiles as it wasn't deep enough, but they would return in the wet season when the water rose.

After a few minutes of pushing through the water, I reached a sandy island mid-stream and couldn't resist sitting down on my pack to take in the scene. Looking back the way I had come, I saw more locals stepping into the water to begin the crossing. I took a drink and some children playing nearby watched me with interest, before they went back into the river, laughing and joking. Pushing my cap under the surface, I replaced it on my head and enjoyed the feeling of the damp material resting on my neck.

Stepping back into the crystal-clear water, I reached a man pushing his old motorbike, piled high with luggage, and helped him towards the other side, wondering if it would start again after all the spray. We came to a young man I had seen on the ridge, who was going in the same direction as us. He asked me where I was headed, as the cool water rippled against my calves.

'Sena,' I told him, knowing that he would know of the town. It was a major settlement and would be a good stopping point on my route before continuing to Caia and the final section of the journey. He nodded and told me that he would help me find the right path. Stepping out of the river bed, we put on our shoes and walked on a dusty path past some giant acacia trees that somehow seemed out of place when everything else was so stunted. We came to a junction and he pointed at the track for me to take, saying he was going to his village which I could see in the distance up a small rise.

Around this point, the Zambezi begins to turn south east and after checking my satnav, I saw that I was a kilometre from the river and set off parallel with it. The path went on and on across flat, stony ground. A small motorbike, chugging with the effort of carrying supplies and belching out dirty exhaust was the only distraction, but it vanished as quickly into the haze as it had arrived.

After a few hours, I noticed through the glare what looked like an old fort up on a hill to my right and went to take a look. Massengano Fort, overlooking the river in the distance, was built by the Portuguese in the seventeenth century to project their power in the area and, crucially, to protect their interests and resupply routes on the Zambezi. The handmade sign at the base of the hill made me smile because it was so basic, but just right for the setting and I wondered what the handful of tourists who visited the fort every year also made of it.

It was quite a climb up to the site and I noticed the impressive fortifications, with walls up to a metre thick in places, built with local stone. It had clearly been built to last and had survived the ravages of time remarkably well. The remains of some of the quarters were still in place and as I wandered around, I thought about the soldiers that had been stationed there, thousands of miles from home, in a hostile environment and having to fight off aggressive tribes. Their hilltop citadel would have given them a sense of security and its views over the surrounding countryside would have allowed notice of impending attack.

Looking around, it was the perfect place to site a fort. On every side, there was a steep and rocky slope below the walls, before the gradient softened and then levelled out a hundred metres below. The Portuguese were known to be excellent engineers and no doubt with the help of local 'pressed' workers, would probably have built the fortification in quick time.

Massengano would have been an interesting place to camp, but I still had distance to cover and besides, there was no water and I wasn't sure what the locals would make of my intrusion. Taking some shade under a spindly tree on the north side, I thought about walking down to the river to see if there was an old dock used to bring supplies to the camp, but decided against it as the heat was pressing and I needed to be on my way. After a final look around and a long, much needed drink of water I clambered back down the hill.

Further on, a cart with a few locals in it pulled by long-horned oxen moved slowly past me. I'm sure it was practical, but it was like a scene from the nineteenth century, before mechanized transport had been invented, and it pressed home how poor the country was.

A little later, the track went past what must have once been a school. The whitewashed single-storey classroom sat forlornly in the sun, with toilet cubicles located to the rear. Peering in through the glassless windows, I saw bricks and broken planks and wondered what had happened to the place. It had perhaps once been a place of learning and giggling children and was now dark and silent.

I had learnt in other parts of Africa that charity groups, desperate to build something tangible rather than just giving money, would sometimes construct a school or clinic in a particular spot, without fully engaging with the locals. Sometimes the structure would be left where it stood, rarely or never being used, allowed to decay and I wondered if that had happened here.

A few hundred metres beyond was a military-looking building of some vintage, with acacia trees growing in the centre, its branches pushing through walls. It must have been from the Portuguese era, like the fort I had seen earlier and been built to last generations. Along the western wall, rising high off the ground, was a row of square openings, like firing points and it looked as though it had been constructed for defence. It seemed a strange location for another small fort, being on flat ground, but it could also have been a government building or merchant's house, built in quieter and safer times.

In the early afternoon, when I was parched and feeling a little weary, I began to look for a village to take some rest. Spotting some men on a path that joined my own, I walked over to them to make some enquiries. Pointing the way they had come, they assured me there was a shop nearby, but I was sceptical as all I could see was a sparsely wooded ridge. I climbed it and then saw the settlement in a bowl, perfectly hidden from the river. It was a Sunday and passing an empty school made of rough red brick buildings, walkways neatly lined with stones, I wondered how many children studied there. A water pump lay broken near some bushes, the rusty iron handle hanging limply to one side and I realised that the villagers probably had to collect their water from the river, a kilometre away.

Coming across a boy of about fourteen, I asked where the banca was and he looked at me with a frown, adamant there wasn't one. I looked enquiringly at him and asked again, but he even pointed back the way I had come. My sixth sense knew that he was lying and I didn't want to give him the satisfaction of making a fool of me. Not being pushed off, I continued on towards some buildings in the centre of the village and after speaking with a few more people, found the shop with little difficulty. I was irritated with the teenager, who didn't want to help me on such a hot day, and wondered why he was like that. Most of the kids I had seen in the country were happy and inquisitive, but this one broke the mould.

Sitting down on a small log in the shade, I enjoyed my Coke as people began to gather around. The teacher was called and asked me some questions and I told him about my trip, which he relayed to the audience, now about thirty locals. Small children pushed their way around the adults for a better look at me and I was pleased to provide some entertainment on their day of rest.

Later, after I had been walking for a few hours without seeing any settlements and was beginning to run out of water, I came across a sandy riverbed and followed it north towards the Zambezi. After a few kilometres following its winding course and then climbing over a small ridge, I saw the river flowing slowly past below me. I had covered over thirty kilometres during the day and was exhausted, pleased to have found such a pleasant spot where I could relax and take the weight off my feet.

Inching slowly down the slope and taking off my pack, I approached the water and something splashed in, probably a monitor lizard judging by the claw marks in the mud. Glancing around, I saw that the locals had burnt the base of some of the trees presumably to try to bring them down and found a ledge above the river to camp on, surrounded by ash.

I put the tent up, gathered some wood for the fire, wandered back down to the river's edge and contemplated a dip. The water was shallow and clear, about a foot deep and in front of me was a small mud island, overgrown with high grasses that reached the shore on either side. It was a mini lagoon and I was about to strip off when I noticed a gap in the vegetation that looked ominous and could have been made by a crocodile. Perhaps my imagination was getting the better of me, already having had a few scares, but I put the dip idea to one side.

Lighting a fire, I heated some water for my dinner and as I was about to taste the first mouthful, a drum began to beat on the other side of the Zambezi. It started off slowly and over time other drums joined in and the sound began to build. It was a wonderful moment, one of the best on the trip, sitting on the riverbank by the fire as darkness descended and hearing the performance across the water. I could still hear the drums later as I drifted off to sleep.

Chapter Eight - The Road to Nowhere

The following morning, I awoke to the sound of birdsong and felt stiff from lying on the solid ground. During the night, when I was half asleep, I had heard a tree creaking before it thumped noisily to the floor. I had pulled myself into a tight ball, expecting a heavy weight to come crashing through the flysheet, but very soon it went quiet and I rolled over, trying to get back to sleep.

When I unzipped my tent at dawn, I found the cause of the disturbance, the tree trunk split in two as one section had fallen towards the river, its branches broken and splintered. Detritus including leaves, vines, twigs and shavings covered the ground close to my tent. I noticed the burn marks around the base of the tree, which must have weakened it over time, causing it to fall.

'Close one,' I muttered to myself as I surveyed the damage.

Packing away my gear, I was annoyed to see that one of my Platypus water bottles had split, soaking some of my clothes. These lightweight bottles are superb for carrying water and fold down small when not in use, and I had used them all over the world without any problems. Heavy use in Mozambique was obviously taking its toll and it reminded me to take better care of my essential equipment. Since nearly running out of water a few weeks before, I knew that I would have to use empty Fizz bottles as containers going forward. I had to begin each day with at least three litres of water, supplemented during the day, to ensure that I never ran out.

Retracing my footsteps to the track, I noticed an encampment that I hadn't seen the previous evening. It was a few hundred metres away and well concealed, but I could clearly see the thorny brush wall surrounding the settlement, with the roofs of the small huts just visible. There was a main entrance along one side and a pile of brush and logs laying to one side, presumably to seal the gap during hours of darkness.

I had seen similar encampments in southern Ethiopia, where locals used them for protection against leopards and hyena. The walls there were made of logs, spiky branches and sticks and had been about six foot high and a few feet thick. As I strode away, I was mystified at the fortifications and wondered what the inhabitants were protecting themselves from. My mind spinning with the thought of predators close by, I hit the track from the day before, turned left and set off into the morning. The thick brush came close to the path on either side and at times it was like walking through a tunnel, the sunlight virtually blocked out.

After a few hours, I came to a small village with huts scattered on a bare hillock and asked hopefully if they had a shop. I thought it would be too small a settlement, but a man beckoned me past some dwellings and pointed to a nondescript place made of mud and logs. The owner was called and after unlocking the padlock, was pleased to sell me a sugary drink and some biscuits.

Some children in torn and grubby clothes had gathered and I wondered why they weren't in school, but realised that they probably had to help with the crops I had seen on the way in. I offered one of the little girls a biscuit and they all stared, as if it was trick, until the selected child reached forward at full stretch and took the gift. Some of the adults chuckled at the response, saying a few words in Portuguese, as the girl looked shyly around, biting on the treat.

Leaving the village, I saw the long, sharp ridgeline that I had heard about in Tete, stretching from left to right in the distance. I headed for the forbidding feature, hoping there was a simple way over it and on towards Tambara, my next waypoint. As I got closer, I could see spindly trees along its length and steep rock walls tumbling down its front.

I came to Chagaca, a well spread out village amongst the trees and the path disappeared. Unable to find anyone to give me directions, and feeling it was unwise to knock on hut doors, I checked my compass and satnav, and set off across waste ground beyond the village. There was no path, just undulating ground baked by the sun with tightly packed and thorny bushes that snagged on my shirt and pack. Taking a compass bearing through the scrub, I walked for a few kilometres before finding a narrow path that led in the general direction I was seeking. Eventually, the trail brought me closer to the rock face which towered over me. Glancing up, I saw sheer rock matted with thorns and knew that even with equipment it would be a tough climb.

Continuing on the path for several kilometres, I eventually came to a bigger track, wide enough for small vehicles, and followed it, hoping it would lead me around the obstacle. I was obviously in a fairly remote area, as I hadn't seen anyone in hours and pressed on in the heat, my cap pulled down hard to prevent sunburn.

The track continued in the right direction for another hour, but then began to turn southwards, away from my desired course. I followed it for a while and then a track of a similar size which was off to my left looked more promising and I took it, assuming it would take me safely over the ridge.

My new route looked perfect. It was going in the right direction, below the cliff and wound its way gently through thick vegetation, rolling with the contours. I congratulated myself on my find by taking a swig of water and resting in the shade for a moment, before setting off again. I walked for another few hours, noticing neatly stacked logs by the side of the track as it began to climb, still winding through brush.

And then it stopped.

I couldn't believe it!

I had invested so much time and energy into the route and couldn't understand why it would just end. I knew I couldn't retrace my steps as I would lose too much time, so I began to search around to see if a path led off into the bush somewhere. After scouring the undergrowth for several minutes, I realised that there was nothing and concluded that I had been on a logging road and once the incline had become too great, its creator had decided to just stop. He could drive the logs out the way I had come in and didn't need to connect with another track further east. The route wasn't on my satnav, nor were there any others within thirty kilometres. I had been keeping my fingers crossed that the track would eventually hit another and take me over the ridge, but my optimism had been poorly placed.

I was annoyed, hot and tired and took a moment to gather my thoughts in some shade. Taking another look around, I understood why the track had ended. Through the trees, I saw not only the rock face that had been on my left for hours, but in the distance another cliff facing me. I had walked into a corner and hadn't seen it coming. Taking out my compass, I thought the best plan would be to plot a route around the cliff to my front and hopefully find a track that would hook round to the east and put me back on track.

Setting off into the head-high scrub, I began to descend and, seeing an overgrown stream bed below me, headed for it. After sliding down a bank, I landed in the rocky bottom and began to make my way slowly along its course. Thick bushes growing across my path were an irritation, clawing at my face and pack, but the route seemed sound, so I stuck with it for about a kilometre, until it began to wind away to the north and away from where I wanted to go.

Climbing out of the stream bed, I forced my way up a slope, with barbs and brambles continuing to catch on my clothes. At times, my pack became so snagged on the thorns that I had to step back and untangle myself. I was worried to see that a tear had appeared on my tent bag that was fastened to the side of my pack and prayed that its contents were undamaged. The tent was my sanctuary and fortress, protecting me from mosquitoes and bugs, and a weakening of that defence was unthinkable.

Reaching the top and walking across a small plateau to the far edge, I was disappointed to see more thick undergrowth below me. One positive fact, though, was that the cliffs had moved further to my left and the ground in front of me was getting flatter. I staggered down through the bush, trying to keep a constant compass bearing and avoid the thorns. At one point, when I ducked under some undergrowth, something landed on the back of my neck and bit me before falling to the floor. Irritated, I strode away and gently touched the bite which had already begun to swell.

'Welcome to Mozambique!' I snapped ironically to myself.

Within minutes, the bite was the size of a small marble and would remain for twenty-four hours, before finally dissipating. Thinking about it later, I had probably disturbed a spider as I went past, its disdain for my being there evident with the bite.

Struggling through the vegetation, I hit another slope and climbed up it, at times on my hands and knees because it was so steep. I grabbed the trunks of small trees to steady my progress and prevent myself slipping back down. Taking a break at the top, I sat on my pack with my navigation aids to reassess my route. I was sure that the bearing was sound and looking down, saw that the terrain was starting to level out even more, although still heavily covered in bushes and thorns. With renewed energy, I traipsed down the slope and picked my way through the undergrowth, making slow but steady progress.

A few hours later, as I took a moment to rest and check my compass, I noticed a pale, straight line about thirty metres away through the scrub, going left to right. Looking closer, I realised it could only be a track and headed for it, thankful to be out of the wilderness. Staggering onto the dusty surface and breathing out a sigh of relief, I began following it east, knowing that I was back on track and able to move faster.

Several kilometres on, I spotted a village some way off and picked up my step to reward myself with a soft drink after my ordeal.

'Banca?' I asked, as I approached a woman bashing something in a bowl.

Shaking her head, she pointed into the distance dismissively and continued with her work. My water bottles were low again and not wishing to put the woman out, I walked a few huts down to a neighbour who gave me as much as I wanted. Not seeing a water pump, I assumed that she had carried it from the river or a pond nearby and told her I was grateful. As I was leaving, five or six dogs which had barked in annoyance at my appearance now followed behind me making sure I left the premises.

Later, the track I was on began to climb through the trees. The rocks and stones made it look like a staircase and the going was difficult. I was convinced there would be a village at the top of the slope and pressed on, wanting to receive my reward of a fizzy drink. But there was nothing at the top, save a downward slope covered in trees. I took a snack out of my pack and consulted my satnav again, but couldn't find any roads or tracks marked, so carried on, using my compass as a guide.

As the light was beginning to fade and I had been moving through unchanging, featureless and spindly woodland for hours, I glimpsed a lone figure in the distance, walking towards me. When we grew closer, I asked him if there was a village nearby where I could stay. Nodding, he guided me along the track and through the trees to a settlement called Djodjo, well spread out on even ground. The man, called Antonio, was a teacher and had been out for a pre-dinner stroll before seeing me approach.

He asked the Mfumu on my behalf if I could camp in the village and after permission had been given, showed me a spot next to his house where I could put up my tent. It was a simple dwelling made of sticks with a thatched roof and had a spindly fence around it, with a cooking area out front in the open. There was a wooden bench by the front door, used for relaxing and eating meals.

As with many villages on my journey, there was no electricity, so the locals only killed the chickens wandering around when they needed them and ate nshima and rice to fill themselves up. A few people were wandering about in the gathering gloom, possibly to chat with a friend or neighbour before darkness took over.

My hands were cut to pieces from scrambling through the undergrowth earlier in the day and I was keen to wash them and apply antiseptic cream to avoid infection. I wasn't particularly hungry, so just made a coffee and sat by the fire with my host, who was interested to hear stories from my journey. He told me that he looked after sixty children at the school a few kilometres away, many of whom had to walk a few hours each day to receive their education. On my travels in Mozambique, I had seen so many young kids and wasn't surprised to learn that women in rural areas had over six children on average, a rate that didn't seem sustainable for such a poor country.

Despite the chill and firm ground I slept well, waking to the sound of dogs fighting nearby. Every village kept them, primarily for protection, and when they bred and their numbers rose, some settlements had become overrun with canine guardians. The dogs were from no discernible breed, but the result of centuries of different types coming together. They were often fawny in colour, some a little darker and had slim, intelligent faces. They were always thin due to a lack of food and would often have 'button ears', where the tips folded over.

As I was packing up, the Mfumu came over with a few others and was fascinated with my lightweight MSR tent, telling the teacher it was a 'magic house'. At only six hundred and fifty grams, it had served me well on the trip, allowing me to move fast, and the headman couldn't believe how light it was when holding it in his hands.

I was away well before seven and walked through the village as people prepared for the day. Cooking fires were burning on either side of me and dogs patrolled. Rejoining the track, I noticed the receding cliffs on my left, which now looked tame and calm in the soft sunlight. The dusty path was tortuous, with little to see on either side, except desiccated brush and trees that hadn't seen rain in months. I wondered what large animals lived out there, if any, and decided there would be few, ones that the hunters had missed.

The track hit numerous junctions along the way and each time I would stop and check my compass before selecting the best option. Sometimes, none of the options looked any good, as out in the wild there were never any signposts and I would just have to use a little reasoning to find the best way. The massive ridgeline, causing me difficulties the previous day, had pushed me miles away from the river and I was determined, even if it was slowly, to edge back towards it.

After four hours on the track and seeing just sand, stones and brush, I arrived at the village of Quasi and sought sanctuary out of the sun. Relishing my drink, I looked around and saw few people, apart from some women with containers on their heads, off to fetch water. I had been told that villagers sometimes had to walk five kilometres to get the liquid when they were far from the river and it was just part of their daily life. Once, earlier in my trip, I had asked why the village couldn't move closer to the water source and was met with a smile and a shrug of the shoulders. The village had been there for a hundred years, I was told, once with its own supply which had now gone dry and it wasn't about to move, even for water.

Leaving the village, I spotted an unsettling shape across the track in the distance. Moving closer, I saw that the serpent was dead, all six foot of it, as ants swarmed around its eyes. It was clearly a black mamba, with its grey body and coffin-shaped head. Even in death it looked sinister and it reminded me to take care when I had to pop into the bushes. It had probably been killed by the village snake patrol the night before and I was surprised it had simply been left there.

Later, I crossed over the large Muira River bed, which was bone dry and offered no opportunity to fill up my water bottles. Soon after, turning north towards the Zambezi, I came to the large village of Togonda, and found a bar selling cold drinks. As the liquid flowed down my throat, I felt energised again and enjoyed the moment to relax.

Setting out for Tambara, I entered the countryside again and after a few hours, whilst I was climbing a hill, a white SUV pulled up next to me. The man, dressed in smart clothes and speaking English, offered me a lift and I politely declined, explaining my reasons. As we were talking, the rear window wound down slowly and a woman in the back, large in body and attitude, said something which made her companion, also a woman of considerable size, titter. No doubt they were amused to find a mzungu toiling in the heat and seemed to be making fun of me whilst they relaxed in air-conditioned luxury.

I covered the miles quickly and in late afternoon came across a banca by the side of the track. Asking if I could camp somewhere, I was taken to the village leader, who gave permission to put up my tent next to some huts. As I was setting up, some chickens were brought over to me and, selecting one and agreeing a price, I put away my pasta and looked forward to a freshly cooked dinner. When it arrived, I tucked into the soft meat with relish, surprising myself with how hungry I was.

Leaving the village the next day, I set out through dry woodland and parched earth that never seemed to change. The terrain had flattened and I was pleased to see the ridges which had caused me so much pain slinking away further to my left. Few settlements touched my route and I had to make do with sips of warm water in the shade, whenever I needed a break.

Arriving in Tambara a few hours later, I walked through the outskirts and saw neat one-storey houses set back from the track. Further in, I came across what looked like government buildings, with official-looking signs pinned to the walls and Mozambican flags hanging limply in the still air. The place was obviously a district centre of some sort, confirmed by the large telecoms tower, bristling with satellite dishes.

I walked on and came to the edge of a hill that looked down on the Zambezi, majestically flowing past in the distance. I hadn't seen the river for a few days and was pleased to see her again in all her glory. At this point, the river was quite wide and I could see a large island midstream, about a kilometre away. Birds were swooping over the water and then flying back to the trees below me.

When David Livingstone travelled through the area there was an abundance of buffaloes and elephants, now sadly gone. He also mentioned the perils of passing through the Lupata Gorge, several kilometres to the west, a narrow defile in which the current flowed so strongly round rocky promontories that the locals were scared of it and placed food on the cliffs nearby as an offering to the gods.

Strolling down the hill towards the river, I passed more government buildings with sleepy-looking officials sitting in the shade. They showed little interest in me as I made my way to the water and past derelict buildings. There were some dugout canoes and boats with outboards tied to the grassy bank and it would have made a great swimming spot to cool off, apart from the presence of crocodiles and Zambezi sharks.

On the road I had been thinking about staying in Tambara, as I was filthy and wanted to sleep in a bed, but there was little to attract me and I didn't make any enquiries about a room. Making my way back up the hill, I stopped and asked some young adults where I could find the *mercado* or market, as I wanted to buy some provisions. The young man, probably about twenty, was with two female friends and he just grinned at me before shrugging his shoulders. 'Mercado' is a common Portuguese word and I said it a few times, trying to enlist his help. He just looked at me and then walked off with his friends, who began laughing, much to my irritation. I had experienced this lack of help to a stranger before and wondered where it stemmed from. It saddened me. I would like to think that if the tables were turned, I would have gone out of my way to help a stranger in my own town.

145

Wandering over to a worker dressed in dungarees next to the telecoms tower, I asked where the market was and he kindly led me to the small supermarket a few hundred metres away, tucked around the corner. As we were walking, I asked him about the route to Sena and he pointed to a track running parallel with the river. I bought a few items, then left the town past some rickety stalls selling biltong, congealing in the heat. They were manned by youths, and I wondered where their future lay. Apparently, fifty percent of the province was below the age of fifteen, as many of the older population were killed in the civil war or died young from natural causes.

After following a monotonous track for much of the afternoon, I arrived at Nyaunga and feeling tired, asked to see the village elder to ask if I could stay. I was led to a circular sitting area, which I learned was called a *baolo* and there were several plastic chairs resting on flattened ground. Around the perimeter and half way up to the thatched roof, rough planks lined the edge. It was obviously his meeting place when conducting business for the village and it could hold about twenty people. Pepe, a teacher with gaps in his teeth, was called over to translate and shortly afterwards the Mfumu arrived, providing me with a warm welcome.

Hearing about my trip, the leader gave permission for me to stay, apparently saying that it would be an honour to host an Englishman in the village. I was tickled at the reference to my own country and wondered if my host had been the recipient of some good will in the past to warrant such a comment. Before entering Mozambique, when Chaz and I had been discussing the trip in Zambia, we had wondered how we might be received by the villagers and had decided, due to their troubled past, that they might be suspicious of outsiders. We had therefore agreed to mainly camp out in the wild, in order to avoid possible confrontation with the locals. My experiences in Mozambique, up to that point, had shown that our thinking had been wrong and that the people were often only too happy to help when a tired traveller passed by.

Taking a rest near Tambara

Relaxing in the shade, I bought the teacher and the Mfumu some soft drinks during our discussion which they seemed to appreciate. As some of the male members of the village gathered in the hut, joined later by children around the edges, I told them about my journey which interested them. The village leader, with greying moustache and blue striped shirt, told me he had fought in the 1972 war against the Portuguese further in the north and had seen many people killed. He also informed me they rarely saw white people in their area, and those they did see raced past in charity SUVs without stopping.

As we continued to talk, I could feel the temperature inside the hut rising as the children on the outside had blocked the airflow. It became quite stifling, as there must have been fifty kids around the outside, listening to the conversation. Thankfully, I was soon able to exit the hut and take some fresh air.

Later, I walked over to Pepe's house, a small brick affair nearby, erected my tent and cooked some pasta on his hot coals in the yard. As I was eating, a drunken man staggered out of the dark to my side, came over to me, shook my hand and began gabbling to me in Portuguese. Explaining that I didn't speak the language, he burped and wandered over to my host who was sitting nearby. The teacher brushed him off and the man swayed back into the dark from whence he came.

Pepe told me that our visitor had recently raped a girl of fourteen from the village and was waiting for the verdict from the court. He also told me that the man had spent time in jail for other offences and was the rogue of the settlement.

'Why isn't he in jail now?' I asked, incredulous.

'Ah, our justice system is very slow and ineffective,' replied my host, glancing at the floor. 'Everyone knows he is guilty.'

'This is awful' I said, shaking my head. 'Where is the girl that he assaulted?'

'Oh, she's over there,' he replied, pointing into the darkness. 'She's OK now and still lives with her parents. The village looks out for her.'

'That's good,' I conceded, shaking my head at the story. 'It must be difficult though, for her to live so close to her attacker?'

'Yes, it must be, but what else can we do? This is her village and this is his village.'

'It's very sad. That guy should be in jail, to give the girl some peace.'

'He should,' replied my host.

Shortly afterwards, I bid Pepe goodnight and slid into my tent. As I closed my eyes, I felt sad that the rapist was still around, living only a few hundred metres from his victim. With the perpetrator's house attached to that of my host and the girl so close, I didn't sleep easily.

In the morning, I woke early and dismantled my tent as

smoke from cooking fires wafted across the village. I was hoping to start walking straight away, but the Mfumu wandered over, plonked his chair on the ground and wanted to brief me on the route. Pepe came to translate and the three of us peered into my satnav device and discussed the villages I would come to, the distances and key features I should know about.

As we were wrapping up, the Mfumu gave me some information he had received from one of the villagers. He told me that a white man, with a pack like mine, had been spotted down by the river the day before and was heading east. It could only have been Chaz following a similar route, going at a similar speed and I was glad he was progressing well.

Chapter Nine - Bandit Country

I rejoined the track and set out towards Chiramba, some forty kilometres away. The road soon reverted to type and wound its way up and down small hills, the trees and vegetation parched and brown. I knew the Zambezi was a few kilometres to my left, but it was out of sight.

Some locals were tending to their crops in an area the size of a football field, pouring water onto plants that looked like carrots. One of the men wore rubber boots. I called a greeting and they smiled shyly back as their bare chests glistened in the heat. Pointing to their water container, I asked where their source was and they pointed towards the river. It would have taken gallons of water to moisten their crop and I marveled at how they just got on with it and kept working.

Coming across some stalls by the side of the road in the early afternoon, I wandered over to see what was for sale. A tarpaulin had been pulled over the display and laid out on trays were hundreds of dry fish neatly laid out in rows. Apart from a few larger specimens, they all seemed to be the same species, about six inches long and quite meaty. I thought about buying a few, as I hadn't had breakfast but despite the best efforts of the stall keeper swatting away at flies with some card, I thought it too much of a risk.

I crossed into Sofala Province and an hour before sunset, the track curled back towards the river and followed alongside. You could smell the Zambezi, earthy and sweet at the same time, as it progressed eastwards towards the ocean. I spotted a communications tower way off in the distance and knew that I had reached the town of Chiramba, clustered back from the water.

Arriving at a Y-junction, I consulted my satnav and decided to stick close to the river. The track led me up a small hill and then curved round towards the heart of the town. I turned and watched the river, sedately moving past, as birds glided over the water and occasionally swooped down to take a drink. I had missed her, trudging along dusty trails all day and was pleased to see her again, glad that she was close.

I had been drinking warm water since morning and craved something different, something cold and with taste. Seeing what looked like a bar close to the water, I headed for it across open ground and found some young women sitting outside, who I learnt later were prostitutes, with babies on the teat. Entering the dark interior, I was pleased to see a fridge humming away merrily in a corner and bought a beer.

As I was handing over some money, one of the working girls from outside sidled up to me, put her arm tenderly over my shoulder and tapped my bottle with her finger, to ask if I would buy her one as well. Shaking my head as politely as I could muster, I stepped into the glare outside and found somewhere to sit on an old concrete ledge.

Enjoying my drink as the river flowed past, I watched a couple of young men in casual wear walk over with their own refreshment and sit down next to me. One of them, who spoke some English, asked where I was heading and not knowing many of the place names in front of me I told him 'Sena', and that I was looking for somewhere to stay. Nodding, he spoke to his friend and said that he would help me find somewhere close by.

As we hit a track heading towards the centre, one of my new companions pointed to some scruffy buildings to the left and I followed him down a narrow path. I assumed he was taking me to somewhere that rented out rooms but as we passed it, it looked like a bordello, with red curtains fluttering gently in the breeze and young women sitting on steps outside and chatting.

Bypassing the distraction, we arrived in a courtyard with policemen relaxing on plastic chairs, pistols on their hips. Those not in uniform, dressed in shorts and sports vests, were kicking a ball around near some trees. The buildings were single-storey, brick-built scruffy affairs, the outsides painted a vanilla colour and the sandy ground around them flattened over time.

For a moment, I wondered if I was taken there to be questioned, but the man who had spoken to me in English turned out to be a policeman and calling to his colleagues, he briefed them on my journey and one by one they walked over and cheerily shook my hand. They were surprised that I was there and I would find out why when I camped at another police station a few days down the road and learned that I was in the middle of bandit country.

After a few minutes of chatting with the policemen, a man of about forty with greying hair came out of the main building and introduced himself as the 'Comandante' (Commander) of the group. He was responsible for the officers there, numbering about twelve, which seemed to me quite high for such an out of the way place. He was happy to see me and seemed impressed with the progress I had made across the country and invited me to camp at the station for the night.

One of the policemen brought me some hot water in a bowl and, retiring to a rundown shower block, I had a wash and a shave which I badly needed. It was so good to be clean again! I was also able to wash a set of trekking gear, covered in grit and grime, and hung it up on a line to dry. Walking back to the sitting area, I was offered a plate of rice, nshima and chicken and tucked in. The food was warm but not hot and I thanked my hosts for the gesture, although I struggled to finish it all. How they survived for months on end on such rations was beyond me, but I suppose with limited resources they had to accept it.

After dinner, one of the policemen feigned interest and took some personal details from me in a notebook, presumably as a record of me passing through for their records, then we sat around chatting. I was interested in the town and what went on there, but my hosts weren't able to tell me much as none were from the area. In Mozambique, policemen are trained in the capital, Maputo, and then deployed to wherever they are needed and not necessarily to their own towns or even regions.

As we talked, the lights went off in the compound and I asked one of the officers about it. He said electricity in Chiramba was erratic, they were without power for several days every week and the police couldn't afford a generator. I was once again staggered that the officers, miles away from home, lived in such poor conditions.

A few of the officers were keen to help me with my tent and laughed as I tried to organise them. They clearly hadn't seen one before and began to pull the material and guide ropes so hard that I thought they were going to tear it. Curbing their enthusiasm, I laid it out on the floor and we put it up slowly, banging pegs into the ground one by one. Once it was up, I sighed with relief.

Some of us then wandered back to the bar I had visited earlier for a nightcap and more chat. I noticed that the prostitutes were still there, but had changed into skimpy dresses, applied copious amounts of makeup and the babies had gone. The young policemen I spoke to seemed bored with their posting and apart from moments of tension and excitement that they wouldn't reveal, their lives sounded dull. That might be why they were so interested in my trip, which gave a taste of adventure they had not experienced. They also loved to talk about English football and knew far more than I did about the premiership, from clubs to players to managers.

I didn't sleep well, as mice or rats were scurrying around the compound for much of the night. All my food and gear was in the tent with me, as always during the hours of darkness, but something must have attracted them, possibly leftovers in the bins nearby.

In the morning, I gathered up my equipment and sat at a table checking out my route, as the officers began to rise, offering greetings. A plate of cold spaghetti arrived in front of me which I politely declined, but it was snapped up by one of the younger men. I couldn't face such unappetizing food first thing in the morning and would buy something on the road, possibly biscuits or fruit. As I was leaving, the

Comandante walked over to me with one of the English-speaking officers.

'You need to move fast out of here, along the river,' I was instructed.

'No problem,' I replied, wondering about the warning and telling him that I was heading for Chemba and hoped to be there before nightfall.

The man slapped me on the back and uttered something to his companion which made him grin.

I imagined he had said, 'Mad Englishman!'

Camping spot at the police station in Chiramba. Bandit country

The wide track led me out of town, past run-down and half-built houses, away from the Zambezi. I was glad that the police had been good enough to give me somewhere to stay. The town was a scruffy place, where not much seemed to happen and there was little evidence of soul, but it had served my purposes well as a waypoint. On his own trip, David Lemon was quite scathing of the settlement:

'Chiramba, which Moffat [one of his guides] had been so keen to reach proved to be a desolate, litter-strewn town that stank to high heaven. The houses were built of brick, but most of them looked derelict and there was nothing to recommend the place so we marched on through.' (3)

A few kilometres out of town I came to a sizeable, brand new bridge with freshly painted blue handrails. Expats in Tete had told me that the Chinese were building bridges all over the country, all in the same design and colours and I wondered if it was part payment for the destruction of the forests. I saw similar bridges over the next few days.

I had set my sights on reaching Chemba, over forty kilometres away but well within my range. On the satnav, the town looked to be quite important, but I had been misled before. The lure of a good meal, cold drinks, a gentle wind blowing off the Zambezi and perhaps a comfortable bed gave me a spring in my step.

After an hour along the winding track in the morning sunshine, it returned to the water, much to my delight. Inland, the route was often monotonous, but by the river there always seemed to be something happening. I would occasionally see fishermen hurling in their nets, or herons patrolling the banks looking for their next meal. I had expected to see hippos on this stretch, as it was sparsely populated, but was lucky if I caught sight of one every few days. Sometimes, I would encounter women in their colourful clothes washing their garments or collecting water, nervously watching as I strolled past.

I passed through a few nondescript villages by the side of the track, amazed to see basic mud huts again that some called home. Electric cables sometimes ran overhead, but these places did not have access to the energy above and the villagers got on with their existence, oblivious to what the power would do to change their lives.

As I approached an acacia tree a little later, I spotted a black and white sign nailed to it and walked over to take a closer look. I had to do a double take, as the rusting image was a warning sign of an elephant and her calf crossing a road. I knew that elephants were found in Mozambique to the north and south of me, but hadn't realised that I could

155

encounter them way outside a national park. I hadn't seen any dung or tracks on my route and wondered if the sign dated from a time of former glory, when the great beasts were common to the area. Shaking my head I carried on, but listening for anything bulky in the vegetation as I walked.

As in other parts of Africa, the elephant population in Mozambique has been decimated, some estimating that the numbers have halved to ten thousand beasts since 2010. They were hunted to virtual extinction for food during the civil war and although their numbers were replenished due to concerted international efforts, they were never safe. The value of ivory to the Far East market directly led to this decline and the slaughter continued. It frustrated me that little action seemed to be taken against those involved in the deadly trade. On his own trek, David Lemon lamented the decline of these majestic animals and was saddened to see only a handful. I had so far seen none.

Passing over hills, which was draining in the heat, I waved to the occasional cyclist burdened by boxes and they would sometimes return my greeting before continuing. The boxes would be stacked on top of one another and were presumably for the village bancas. Except in Tete, I hadn't witnessed any organised form of resupply in the country and put it down to the lack of decent roads and willingness to invest in such a scheme. My fellow travellers often wore old coats or jumpers, as I had seen in other parts of Africa, when I wore just thin lightweight trousers and shirt.

In mid-afternoon, near Goba, I came across a lovely pond alongside the track, about the size of a tennis court, and paused to admire it. It was deep in places, the clear water showing the small fish swimming past and vegetation on the bottom. The Zambezi was a few kilometres away and I considered a quick dip to cool me down, but then realised that as a permanent water source it might have large, toothy residents and decided against it. The sheer joy of lowering a sweaty body into cool water is difficult to match, but the risk was too great and I ambled past, longingly watching the water.

As I marched up the inclines, along the flat and down the descents, I felt truly fit and strong. My trek across northern Spain a few months earlier had prepared me well and I was now covering over thirty kilometres a day, sometimes more. My feet were unblistered and tough and my legs were as strong as tree trunks. It was good to travel at my own pace, stopping when I wanted and pushing on when I chose. I had the luxury of walking solo, unencumbered by baggage trains and companions. On his expedition along the Zambezi, David Livingstone noted that his party averaged from two to two and a half miles an hour in a straight line and rarely marched for more than six hours per day. The reason for this was:

'This in a hot climate is as much as a man can accomplish without being oppressed; and we always tried to make our progress more a pleasure than a toil'. (1)

A few hours later, I reached the outskirts of Chemba and briefly watched a game of football taking place on a makeshift pitch. The teenagers were going at it with a vengeance, but displayed more enthusiasm than skill. It was good to see them playing some sport and enjoying themselves, when there seemed little else to keep them occupied.

Further on, in a beautiful lagoon parallel with the track, women were dipping their clothes into the water and vigorously rubbing them with bars of soap. Plastic baskets of freshly washed garments were sitting on the bank, waiting to be carried home. It looked another great swimming spot after a hard day on the road, but being open to the river made it unsafe.

Chemba was quite a big settlement, the main one in the four thousand square kilometre Chemba District, and I wondered what I would find. As darkness began to fall, I climbed a hill into town, passing a few drunks on the way. Running along the side of the track was an old graveyard partly hidden by trees and brush, and I wondered if the occupants were early Portuguese settlers who had succumbed to the dangers of the country. The gravestones were ornate and impressive, some surrounded by rusting metal chains and they looked expensive, probably beyond the means of locals.

As I walked, I noticed some small houses had lights above the doors hinting at development and it was good to see that the town had reached the electric age. Thin and patchy curtains hung across the glass, providing a semblance of privacy and I wondered what the furnishings would be like inside. I had stayed in similar homes on the trek across Zambia where they were simple affairs with old furniture, dusty interiors and little natural light. The kitchens were basic but functional and the toilet and wash room would be another hut close by.

Arriving at a junction, I asked a couple of teenage boys where I might get a cerveja and was pointed to a brightly lit building a few hundred metres away. I was parched from the heat of the day and needed to clear the dust from my throat. The place was basic, with plastic chairs arranged around a table under a makeshift corrugated iron roof, but they had cold beer. Taking a sip from the bottle, I enjoyed the sensation of cold liquid hitting the back of my throat and twirled the fluid around my mouth to prolong it. I asked the man at the bar if he served food, but he shook his head dismissively and gestured down the road towards the brighter lights of the town centre.

I persuaded him to show me where the police station was, to see if I could camp in the compound. Though it was not something I had considered prior to the journey, staying with the police seemed like a good idea as it offered the weary traveller some protection and interesting conversation and I thought I would try my luck again.

Stepping into a large, unlit walled compound, we stumbled through the darkness in what resembled a building site. There were piles of bricks, pieces of wood and loose wire everywhere and I wondered if we had the right place.

Eventually, we arrived at a small office with a single bulb hanging forlornly from the ceiling and the Comandante was called.

I was expecting an older man to appear, but a young officer in his mid-twenties with pristine uniform and gun on his belt strode in with a flurry of self-importance and took a seat behind the desk. I asked if he was the commander and he assured me he was, as he studied my dirty clothes with interest.

In my best sign language and hand gestures, I explained my journey to the policeman and asked if I could put my tent up in the compound. My request was met with a stern face and a flat refusal, as the man explained that there was no room in the compound. I told him I only needed a bit of flat ground and that I would be gone by morning, but he raised his voice and pointed to the exit. Thanking him all the same and pulling my pack back on, I made my way into the night as I plotted plan B.

Trudging into the centre of town, slightly annoyed, I reflected on the Comandante's decision. I would have thought the authorities would want to ensure the safe transit of visitors through their area, particularly white ones, when Mozambique was so devoid of visitors, especially here in the north. I concluded that he was standing in for the real boss and wanted to show how decisive he was. I put his thinking down to his youth, where he hadn't learnt that he could be flexible with his power.

Chemba had begun life as a native village, but the Portuguese developed it into a town due to its close proximity to the Zambezi River and usefulness as a centre for trade. I was shocked to discover later that ninety per cent of the people in the district were illiterate and that only ten per cent could speak Portuguese, a damning indictment on the standard of education in the country.

The main street looked like something out of a cheap Western with a sandy cambered surface overlooked by ramshackle two-storeyed buildings. Open drains next to the

159

road were full of rubbish, and stray dogs with scarred faces patrolled nearby. I knew I wasn't going to find a restaurant of Gordon Ramsay quality, but I was starving and needed to eat and build up my strength. I had already lost weight on the journey and didn't want to arrive at the ocean as skin and bones.

I found a place by asking around and was led past some shacks into a dingy room, lit only by a drinks fridge, with a few other diners. The tables had colourful plastic covers, which hadn't seen a clean for some time, the pictures of flowers disguising old crumbs. Looking around, I considered leaving to go and boil up some water for my pasta, but decided against it when a beer was brought to my table. After some time, a waiter sauntered over and if I was expecting a choice of food, I was to be disappointed. I asked him what they had and he pointed to a table nearby, where there were plates of rice and fish that looked grey in the gloom.

'Looks wonderful!' I said sarcastically, as the man disappeared into the darkness towards the kitchen.

Another beer on an empty stomach obviously muddled my brain, as when the food eventually arrived it actually tasted quite good. It wasn't hot but warmish and the fish was bony and plain, but for the equivalent of two pounds it was good value and anyway, I was ravenous.

Before the trip, I had been worried about possible food poisoning, as I had witnessed kitchen hygiene in numerous African countries before and knew it was easy to get sick. So far in Mozambique, though, I had been relatively fortunate when eating in local places and apart from the odd hiccup had stayed healthy.

Suitably fed and watered with the best Chemba could offer, I made my way out of town to find somewhere to sleep. Finding a track that appeared to be going east, I followed it, ignoring the shouts and taunts from drunks in the bars I passed by. As the buildings began to disappear, I noticed some streetlights off to my left in the distance and walked towards them, thinking it was the road to Sena. As I stumbled over waste ground, littered with gullies and holes, a container lorry trundled along the row of lights and I knew my assumption had been correct.

Walking away from the light, I found a flat area and, working quickly, erected my tent and slid inside. I assumed there would be dwellings nearby, although I hadn't seen any cooking fires, and didn't want to be disturbed if I was noticed. It was quite a warm evening and I didn't need my sleeping bag liner, but slept in my clothes in case I needed a quick getaway.

I woke early in the morning to the sound of a dog barking near my tent and turned over to try to catch more sleep, thinking it was just a stray. A little later, I heard the dog again, but this time it was growling in an inquisitive way and sounded closer. I then heard muffled voices and some subdued laughter and knew that my rest was over.

'Mzungu!' I called through the fabric, letting my visitors know who I was.

Unzipping the tent, I peered outside and found about forty people of all ages standing there looking at me. Some were staring, some grinning, whilst others chatted nervously to their neighbour. My shelter was obviously a strange sight for them and they must have been confused as to what it was.

'Morning!' I said cheerily, followed by 'Bom dia!' and was pleased to see nods and smiles.

Looking around, I noticed simple huts on higher ground in the distance, probably where these people lived. A young man stepped forward and asked me in broken English where I had come from. I told him Zumbo, which he relayed back to the crowd, who chuckled in amusement. As I was low on water, I asked one of the young boys standing nearby if he could fill up my bottle and he jogged away in the direction of the huts.

Pulling down my tent, I asked my audience about the route to Sena and they all pointed to the road I had seen the night before and broke into more smiles and chuckles. My Sygic navigation system told me that the town was forty kilometres away and I knew I could cover the distance in a day.

Waving goodbye to my new friends, I stepped onto the road as the sun rose higher on the horizon. I felt good after some decent food and a night's rest, and was looking forward to another day on my journey.

On the outskirts of town I passed the secondary school, dedicated to a woman called Teresinha with a wonderful picture of her painted on the exterior wall. The place of learning looked immaculate with well-maintained buildings and trees in tidy rows, and not a piece of litter to be seen. The school head obviously had high standards and I hoped the children appreciated it, when I had seen other places of education falling to ruin.

After an hour, needing to recharge my phone battery and power pack, which hadn't been plugged in since Tete, and not knowing when I would get the opportunity in the near future, I stopped at a shop by the side of the road. Taking advantage of their multi-plug power lead, I was able to relax, knowing that I would be set for at least a few days. The owner seemed happy enough, as I was buying drinks whilst I was there for the hour.

I had decided to head for Villa de Senna (known locally as Sena), as I heard it was a major town. Every so often, as my route crested a hill or turned a corner, I caught a glimpse of the Zambezi in the distance, still flowing gently to the sea. Then, as the track skirted a hill, I lost sight of the water and wouldn't see it again for several hours.

Passing through the small settlement of Pungo and minding my own business, I spotted some young men in the distance sitting in the shade next to a banca. As I got closer, one of them lowered his bottle to the floor and ran across the track towards me, watched by his amused friends. Screeching to a halt in front of me, the man asked something in Portuguese, to which I shrugged my shoulders and walked on. He was clearly intoxicated, the drink no doubt giving him the courage to be a pseudo official for the day and he jogged back in front of me, trying to block my path. Not interested in playing his game, I walked around him and pointed down the road and said, 'Sena'. I heard a few more words of Portuguese behind me and some laughter from the direction of the banca, but ignored them and kept going.

In the late morning, as I strolled along a sheltered part of the road, I noticed tall green crops growing to the left of me, in what looked to be massive circles. As I studied them, the crops would slowly bend away as an edge to the circle, disappearing towards the river. I had seen these when discussing the route with Rudi's friend Donald, back in Tete. Clustered together and up to a kilometre in diameter, these strange circles were probably the site of some kind of experimental farm.

Later, crossing over a small bridge, I came to the sign for Caia district and felt pleased with the progress. The town of Caia was still seventy kilometres away but it felt good to be on track and I took a quick rest to celebrate.

I was on the go for most of the day and by sunset I was shattered. The first clue that I was nearing Sena were the lights on the Dona Ana railway bridge that crossed the Zambezi way off to my left. Built by the Portuguese in 1934, it connects the town with Mutarara on the north bank and was built for road use, but converted for rail a few decades later. It spans more than three kilometres over the river and is the largest bridge in southern Africa. Although sabotaged by South African Special Forces during the civil war, it was rebuilt once hostilities had ended. The railway that crosses the bridge does not carry passengers, but is primarily used to transport coal from Tete to the coast, a few hundred kilometres away.

Shortly after passing the bridge, I saw a telecoms tower, which I presumed was in the town, with beacons on top, showing me the way. It was a long walk into the heart of the place and I passed simple homes set back from the road, some with little vegetable patches out front. David Livingstone described the town as:

'…being built on a low plain, on the right (south) bank of the Zambezi, with some pretty detached hills in the background and surrounded by a stockade of living trees to protect its inhabitants from their troublesome and rebellious neighbours.' (1)

Arriving in the hustle and bustle of the centre, I found a shop down a side street that sold cold drinks and sat on a bench outside, relishing my reward. Locals wandered around in front of me with curious looks on their faces. I asked the shopkeeper if there was anywhere to stay in town and leaving someone to guard his wares, he led me to a few places. The rooms had no windows and no running water and the dirty sheets were rumpled on the bed, as if the previous occupant had just walked out. All rooms had mosquitoes hanging ominously from the ceilings, a sign that an uncomfortable night came as part of the package. I had avoided malaria so far in Mozambique and didn't want to catch it now. The toilet areas were filthy and smelt of urine. I decided that I would be far better off sleeping in the bush. Shaking my head and wondering why standards had to be so low, I headed back towards the bright lights of the centre.

I was starving, having not eaten much all day, and crossed hopefully over to the market. Wandering around the rickety stalls, I saw cuts of meat sitting on dirty cardboard and bunches of bananas that had seen better days, and was amazed that the quality of food was so bad in such a large town. I had been looking forward to reaching Sena all day, expecting to find decent food and somewhere acceptable to stay, but my optimism was dwindling rapidly.

Eventually, I found a girl no older than ten cooking vegetable samosas in a little fryer and bought a few, sitting down on my pack to eat them. A group of young teenagers with surly faces gathered around me and I wondered if they were going to cause trouble, but they just gawped at me, exchanging comments with each other as I ate. The samosas were piping hot but there were few vegetables inside. It was hardly fine dining, but I was grateful that I had at least found something to put into my empty stomach.

Realising there was little left to interest me, I strolled out of town, hoping to find another food stall on the way, but there was nothing, only seedy bars and small shops selling vehicle batteries, tyres and engine oil. When the streetlights abruptly ended, I kept going but was startled when my foot hit something solid on the road and a dog leapt to its feet and scurried away, emitting low growls as it went. The poor thing had obviously been sleeping on the track and only woke up when my shoe collided with it, giving both of us a fright. I could just make out its outline by some bushes as I passed, hearing more growls of annoyance, and left it alone to find its next sleeping spot.

When travelling near Sena, David Livingstone had his own difficulties when his support vessel the Ma Robert, which helped to shuttle supplies for the expedition along the river, came to an untimely end:

'…the leaking vessel ground finally on a sandbank and immediately filled with water. She could neither be pumped out or floated off. During the night the river rose and the next day all that was visible of the wreck was the top six feet of her two masts. Most of the goods on board were saved and removed to an island…till rescued by canoes sent from Sena by the friendly Senhor Ferrao'. (2)

Glancing from left to right, I could still see dwellings in the darkness and pressed on, not wanting to camp in someone's garden. About a kilometre further on, beyond the edge of town, as the road began to turn and my eyelids were getting heavier, a figure emerged from the darkness quite close to me, making my heart skip a beat.

Quickly turning on my headtorch, I saw a vagrant dressed in rags, shielding his eyes from the light. He looked about thirty, although it was difficult to tell due to his wildly frizzy hair and scraggly beard, covered in grime. His trousers, torn to the knee on both legs, were stained dark brown and his shirt, a similar shade and a few sizes too small, was held closed by just a few buttons.

'Ola!' (hello) I called out in greeting, once I had recovered from my shock, but he just looked at me, scratching his face and blinking in the light.

The stranger was obviously down on his luck and possibly an outcast from the town. I had heard that young men who caused trouble with their families, or committed crimes that never reached the police, were sometimes discarded by their communities to live a life in the countryside, where they would end their days. The man's feet were shoeless, cut and filthy and I noticed him clasp his hands tightly together and bow his head as if he had nothing left. I guessed that he had avoided 'village justice,' still common in some parts of Africa, where the perpetrator could be beaten to death with clubs, stoned or even have tyres placed over their necks and set alight.

'Ola!' I repeated in a quieter tone, letting him know I wasn't a threat and meant him no harm.

Raising his head, he continued to just stare into the light, his eyes empty and worn. Giving him a wide berth, I still caught a smell of the man and knew that he hadn't seen soap in years. Setting off quickly again, I was keen to find a campsite and rest up for the night.

After a few minutes of trudging through the darkness, my pace slowed when I realised that I was being followed. After the fright, my senses were fully tuned to the environment and I could hear the unmistakable sound of the soft padding of footsteps behind me.

Turning around, I flicked on my torch and saw the man who had also stopped, at the limit of the beam, looking towards me. I didn't feel threatened, as he seemed so wretched and lost and I just felt sorry for him. I watched him for a few moments in the torchlight, his figure still as stone, and headed slowly away again, stopping every few minutes to listen and check that he wasn't there.

By now I was deadly tired and walking on for another few kilometres to put some distance between me and the vagrant, I began to look for somewhere to sleep. Before turning on my torch to inspect the ground, I sat down on my pack and looked the way I had come, swiveling my ears to catch any sound. Satisfied that the outcast had stayed closer to town, I switched on my torch to check for snakes and find a pitch. I found a suitable flat spot near some bushes about a hundred metres from the track. The mosquitoes had started to bite and I was desperate to get away from them and rest. Using my torch as sparingly as possible, I quickly erected the tent and slipped inside, hoping the vagrant hadn't followed me from a distance and caught sight of my light.

When David Livingstone passed through the area, he had mentioned the numerous lions that lived there and, having been attacked and nearly killed by one on an earlier expedition in neighbouring South Africa, he knew of the danger. The lions have now gone from the area around Sena, but I was uneasy from my encounter. It had been a long day with little reward and despite my worry, I was asleep within minutes.

Chapter Ten - Heartbreak Road

I awoke to the sound of people moving through the bush around me and shouted out 'Mzungu!' to let them know who I was. I could hear titters as they got on with their day, no doubt amused that a white man had slept there. Rolling over, I slept a little more until the first rays of sun were hitting the tent and I knew I had to raise myself.

Stepping out of my shelter, I saw the path that my visitors had used, which I hadn't spotted in the darkness. It led down towards the river, about a kilometre away and I guessed they were collecting water or washing their clothes.

I rarely had breakfast when staying in the bush, except when I found a camping spot concealed from the locals. Normally, like today, I would pack up quickly and get on the road to avoid any potential trouble. My first meal of the day would often consist of biscuits or fruit, taken a few hours along the way.

The railway that I had crossed in Sena was a hundred metres to my right and I walked parallel with it for several kilometres before crossing back over it at a simple level crossing and then having it on my left. No trains ever passed me and I learnt later that the route was used infrequently to carry coal from Tete to the coast. I then began what I termed 'Heartbreak Road' that stretched into the distance, never deviating its course and going on for hours. The track had turned from brown to grey and was covered in sharp stones that cut into the rubber of my shoes and I wondered if the tyre repair shops in the area did a roaring trade.

Later on, I spotted strange shapes erupting out of the ground and wandered over for a closer look. They were giant anthills, over ten feet tall, with vegetation growing up the sides. Some went straight up, whilst others leaned over at strange angles and one was even an 'r' shape. The inside of the structure is apparently designed to keep the workers, queen and eggs cool in hot climates and I was impressed with their engineering efforts. The surface was rough to the touch and as hard as concrete and looked more substantial than many of the homes I had passed that morning.

Needing a break mid-morning, I stopped at a fruit stand and bought bananas and a papaya. I pulled out my knife, found a log to sit on and began to carve up the foot-long papaya, watched with interest by the locals. It was succulent and sweet and perfect for a baking hot day and I ate the whole thing, as juice ran down my fingers. Then the strangest thing happened. As I was putting away my knife and looking around, a young girl of about ten walked over to me, curtsied and handed me a tissue to wipe my fingers. It was an act of such kindness that I hadn't experienced in recent days and I gave her my best smile in appreciation.

Back on the road, I walked onwards, pleased by the encounter and hoping to have similar experiences later in the journey. An hour later, I passed a large pond on my right near the settlement of Juzi, with part of it disappearing behind lush grass and reeds. It looked so out of place that I had to stop. For hours I had been toiling through the heat and passing through desiccated bush, with not an inch of green to be seen and here was an oasis in the middle of nowhere. Young boys were splashing about in the water and shrieking in joy to each other, taking advantage of a freak in geography. I wasn't sure how the pond had come into existence but it looked well established and was obviously appreciated.

I had been trudging for hours along a particularly straight section of Heartbreak Road, my concentration wavering due the heat and sweat dripping down into my eyes, when in the distance I saw a car approaching fast, a dust cloud bellowing behind it. On my side of the track there was thick thorny brush, not the place to step into for safety and I studied the approaching vehicle keenly to see if it would move into the centre of the road to avoid me.

Moving slowly forwards, my eyes never left the hurtling object. I wasn't sure if the driver had seen me, though I assumed I would stand out against the pale background, but

I moved away from the verge nevertheless and began to wave my arm in a gesture for him to stay clear. The car, however, kept its course and as it bore down on me rapidly, I desperately looked for somewhere to step off the road. At the last second, I pushed myself into the thorns and faced the vehicle, wondering who the lunatic driver was. As it flashed past inches from me, I saw four men inside, all wearing Islamic taqiyah skullcaps and scornful looks.

Stepping back onto the track a little shaken, I held out my hands at the disappearing vehicle, as if to say, 'What was that all about?' as it roared off into the distance. I shook my head and began to brush the dust from my clothes. It was strange that the driver hadn't moved to avoid me when I had made myself visible. Perhaps it was the colour of my skin or wrong religion that had offended the men, but it played on my mind for hours. Islam is strong along the coastal belt of Mozambique, having established itself as early as the twelfth century along with trading posts to move ivory, slaves, gold and other precious goods back to the Middle East. I didn't want a repeat performance.

Towards the end of the afternoon, strong winds suddenly picked up from nowhere and I was blown about as I tried to maintain my course. Grit and silt blew into my eyes and it was difficult to keep an eye on the road, where vehicles continued to race past.

Later, I passed a football game where two sides were battling it out in front of an enthusiastic crowd of hundreds. It was a Sunday and obviously a good opportunity to get teams together to compete. The players were wearing normal clothes, trousers, shirts and normal shoes and didn't seem disadvantaged with a lack of gear. The ball travelled repeatedly and speedily from one end to the other and I felt tired just watching. There were no drink stands, food stalls or snack bars and I thought that a local entrepreneur was missing an opportunity.

Arriving in a small place called Murraca an hour later, I spotted a roadside drink stall and walked over. A policeman was enjoying a Coke in the shade and, buying one too, I took the weight off my feet and sat next to him. After a few minutes of chat, limited because we didn't speak each other's language, I noticed the police station further down the road and asked the officer in sign language and gestures if I could stay. He nodded his head without hesitation and called a friend over who could speak some English. I asked the new officer the same question and he replied, 'Of course!' as if it happened every day and was no big deal. I thanked him and bought a round of drinks in appreciation, as the man asked about my journey and told me about the town.

At the police station, I was shown into a large room at the side. There was a motorbike parked there and a few sleeping mats on the floor and I was given a spot in the corner. Taking a quick wash in the yard, I was disturbed by vervet monkeys playing in the trees nearby, swinging from branch to branch. Putting aside my soap and flannel, I strolled over to the tree and looked up at the interlopers. On seeing me they stopped their play and stared downwards, moving their heads to get a better look. I hadn't seen monkeys since west of Tete and it was good to have their company again.

Finishing my ablutions, I returned to the front of the building to find a local slumped in the dirt by the steps.

'What happened to him?' I asked an officer.

'Oh, he has been fighting,' he replied, clenching his fists and imitating a boxing action.

I put the unfortunate in a recovery position, noticing his badly swollen and cut lip, along with the stench of beer. The policemen didn't seem very concerned about their new charge and just chatted amongst themselves.

'Is there a doctor or nurse to help him?' I asked.

'No. No doctor. We have called his family to take him away. They will look after him.'

Soon afterwards, as the light began to fade, an older man on a motorbike rode up and spoke with the officers. With difficulty, they picked up the limp figure and hauled him onto the bike, making him sit, then wrapped his arms around the older man, who turned out to be his father and shouted instructions to the drunk, who burbled in response. The bike moved off slowly, back towards the road, with the father trying to keep it stable as the drunkard's head lolled from side to side. I asked if it was common for drunks to arrive at the station in that state and learned that it was. Apparently, the young men of the town, having worked hard all week, spent all their money on beer and started fighting at any provocation.

After all the excitement, I wandered over to the drink stall and had a few beers with the policemen, some of them still in uniform. They asked me about my route and I mentioned the towns I had passed through since leaving Tete. Incredulous, they checked the route with me again and the man who spoke some English turned to me and smiled.

'You are lucky! That road is dangerous, we have *banditos* there!'

He told me the group of bandits robbed travellers on the road and the local police had been called in to try to put a stop to it. The bandits were aligned to the Renamo Group and had even attacked the town of Chiramba in 2016. They had taken over the police station where I had stayed, stolen all the medical supplies from the clinic and forced out those who didn't agree with their way of thinking. Much of the population had fled into the bush or taken sanctuary on some islands on the Zambezi, and needed a great deal of encouragement from the authorities to return to their homes. A large police force had been sent into the area, which forced the men out of the town, but they had remained in the vicinity, causing problems to travellers on the road ever since.

That was why there had been so many policemen in the Chiramba station and I thanked my luck for getting through unscathed. Back in Zambia, when Chaz and I were walking towards Mozambique, we had come up with scenarios of problems we might face including robbers on the road, and agreed on a course of action if this occurred. Thankfully it hadn't. Now on my own, I would have been in a tight spot had banditos appeared.

As we were drinking, some female students from the local college, who lived behind the drink shop, wandered over and were persuaded to dance for us. A policeman sitting next to me winked and told me that one of the dancers was his girlfriend. As they jigged in front of our seats, heads, arms and bodies going everywhere, their audience clapped and shouted enthusiastically in appreciation. It was a very vibrant sight with feet pounding into the earth and great to watch. I was even persuaded to join them, despite my tiredness, much to the merriment of my hosts. All my aches and pains of carrying a pack in the heat along Heartbreak Road were put aside as I enjoyed the moment.

A police commander passing in his car bought more beer for his officers, which was shared around, and I was glad there wasn't a major incident requiring their attention. Leaving the party well before it had finished, I made my way back to the station to make some dinner and prepare for bed.

Across the Zambezi from here was the Shire River tributary that David Livingstone had travelled up as part of the main expedition. On it, he discovered Lake Nyassa (now Lake Malawi) when trying to find another water route into Central Africa, but it continued north and he returned to the Zambezi downhearted. It staggered me how much distance he had covered, albeit with companions, in hostile terrain and with rudimentary equipment. One such encounter related by Martelli indicated how dangerous it could be when Livingstone's party was attacked from the bank of the river by a large body of tribesmen firing muskets and arrows. Apparently, some bullets passed through the sail of his boat, whereupon one of his companions shot dead a man who was 150 yards away. A second attacker was killed shortly afterwards.

Thankfully, the only hostility for me was from mosquitoes. After crawling into my liner on top of my defunct sleeping mat and applying some mosquito repellent,

I listened to the merriment outside before falling into a deep sleep.

I woke the next morning and, running my fingers around my neck, discovered the bites I had received in the night. The mosquitoes had got through my defences and enjoyed themselves, but probably also had a hangover, judging by the amount of beer I had drunk the night before.

Saying goodbye to the officers, I stepped on to the road in the morning light and walked through the rest of town and on towards Caia. On the outskirts was a wonderful old building at the end of a driveway. In the expansive grounds, well-kept and orderly, tall palm trees swayed in the gentle breeze. Schoolchildren in neat and clean uniforms, with satchels over their shoulders, were ambling in to their lessons. I wondered where their futures lay. The literacy rate in Mozambique is poor, with only one in two adults able to read in the country as a whole, with much lower figures in the regions, and very few making it to university. Was I looking at the country's next scientists, lawyers or businessmen, or the next generation of stall holders, cleaners or farmers, destined never to leave the town?

Passing more children on the road chatting away with their friends, I saw fields of crops more organised than before. What looked like sugar cane was growing close to the verge and men, already sweaty from the exertion, were flailing machetes and stacking it in bundles. The cane looked a perfect habitat for snakes: dark, cool and no doubt with an abundance of rodents. Not envying their labours, I wondered how many of the men were bitten every year.

I reached the outskirts of Caia by noon and walked past simple brick houses and makeshift bars by the side of the road. Music blared out from these drinking dens and figures slumped in the shade, clutching their bottles. The outskirts seemed to go on forever, the view never changing: more simple houses and more bars, musically competing with each other. Caia and the surrounding communities, I knew, was experiencing an HIV/AIDS epidemic due to poor education

174

and knowledge about the disease, and had attracted international support to try to slow its progression. I noticed that some of the people, particularly the women, looked painfully thin and the stretched and discoloured skin on their faces hinted at the illness. Similar to other provinces along the Zambezi, half of the population was under fifteen, many adults having been taken by AIDS before they reached their thirties.

Finding a quiet place to rest, I bought a cold drink and sat in the shade, watching the world go by. A few cars trundled past, but the majority of people were on foot, going about their business. Some of the men walked purposefully along wearing old suit jackets and carrying tools, whilst children strolled past, their minds otherwise engaged. Women were often carrying bags of vegetables on their heads, heading home to prepare the meals for later.

The track I was on eventually hit the tarmac road and I headed for the main part of town and the bridge beyond. It went from being relatively calm to frenetic in seconds, as trucks and cars flashed past me, shaking my senses. I had been on a long, straight track for days, where the traffic had been light and easy to see as it approached. Now, I was back in what felt like a city: noisy, dirty and teeming with people. Breathing in exhaust fumes, I passed shops selling basic goods from car batteries and tyres to plastic furniture and cloth.

Wanting to rest before crossing the river, I found a decent looking place called Rochas, walked up the steps and ordered a beer. A few other guests in smart-casual clothes were sitting in the shade of the wide fronted building. Life-sized swans made of concrete graced the steps of the main entrance. In a developed country people would have sniffed at the sculptures, but here in Caia, they seemed to fit in and gave the establishment some class.

I knew that this would be the last major town before hitting the ocean, so it felt good to relax and watch the world go by. I've never been a fan of sprawling towns and cities, preferring the calm and tranquillity of the countryside, but in Mozambique the hustle and bustle gave me some security, when many of the dangers were outside.

I would probably pass through Caia on my return from the ocean and was pleased to see the bus station opposite to where I was sitting. With any luck, I would be sitting in the same spot in about a week, waiting for my own departure. Full minibuses were pulling up and disgorging their loads, whilst others began to quickly fill. Young men, looking older probably than their years, were patrolling the forecourt anxiously looking for new passengers, and organised the departures with enthusiastic shouts and arm-waving.

Feeling hungry, I wandered into the restaurant and studied the display boards behind the counter. There were items upon items to choose from and photographs of selected dishes to whet the appetite. My eyes latched onto something I hadn't eaten for ages and walking to a table, I sat down in anticipation. When the beef burger and chips arrived over half an hour later, I grinned from ear to ear.

For weeks I had been eating pasta and soup, interspersed with the occasional chicken, piece of fruit or portion of street food and now I fully understood the concept of 'comfort food'. Biting into the hot burger brought joy beyond measure and I didn't want the moment to end. Dipping recently fried chips into ketchup brought equal pleasure and once the meal was complete I just sat there in total bliss. Still on a high from the culinary experience, I considered ordering the same again, but knowing how long the first had taken, decided against it. As I relaxed at my table and enjoyed the comfortable setting, a well-dressed young local came up and asked me in English where I was going.

'Chinde,' I replied with a grin on my face.

'Can you repeat that?' he asked.

'I'm going to Chinde. It's the final stop on my journey along the Zambezi.'

The man looked at me unsurely, as though I was making fun of him, but I assured him that I was telling the truth and we began to talk about my journey. He introduced himself as Pablo and after a while he shook his head and told me that I was crazy and I nodded as if to agree. He owned a shop nearby selling electric goods and he was clearly doing well, judging by his watch, phone, gold jewellery and smart clothes.

'Have you been to Chinde?' I asked him.

'No, no,' he replied. 'I wouldn't go down there. This is my town and I'll die here.'

'Have you travelled much around the country?'

'Some places. Tete, Sena, Beira. I go to fetch supplies for the shop.'

I nodded, a little sad that my new friend hadn't seen much of his own country, but conscious of his circumstances. After further conversation, he returned to his shop, wishing me luck for the rest of my journey.

I knew I had to get going, as I still had to cross the massive bridge over the Zambezi and find somewhere to stay, but I felt so comfortable in my chair that I was reluctant to leave. Checking my satnav again, I knew I had no option but to cross the river, as the track on the southern bank seemed to run out long before the ocean and I didn't relish traversing through marshy wilderness in the latter stages of the journey. The area was so vast, the size of Cyprus, that you could disappear in there and it would take days to retrace your steps and return to Caia.

Finally leaving the restaurant, I passed an amputee sitting on a cart of rough-hewn wood, its rusty wheels from an old pram. The man's legs ended mid-thigh and I tried to put out of my mind the terrible pain he must have suffered. He looked like another mine victim from the war and I wondered where he had fought and nearly lost his life. He was selling lotto cards balanced on his contraption, and I marveled at how he endured every day.

Leaving some money on the cart, I walked towards the bridge, spotting its steel arches way in the distance. It was further away than I had thought and after an hour plodding along a straight road, I reached the start of it, a barrier pole blocking access on both lanes and a few minibuses waiting to cross. Professional-looking and muscle-bound soldiers with AK-47s slung over their shoulders and dressed in camouflage uniforms were checking documents and scanning around for trouble. These were no ordinary troops; these were specialist in nature, protecting a national asset. I could understand the show of force. As one of the few crossing points over the Zambezi in Mozambique, it controlled access to the north and south of the country and was very much of strategic importance.

A soldier came up and asked for my passport and after a brief flip through the pages, handed it back and allowed me to proceed. The Armando Emilio Guebuza Bridge, opened in 2009, is over two kilometres long and is said to be the pride and joy of the president, after whom it is named. Replacing a basic ferry service for vehicles and people, it was constructed to generate development in one of the poorest provinces in the country. Lorries can now pass through the east of the country from Tanzania to southern Mozambique, while before they had to travel two hundred and fifty kilometres west, crossing the river at Tete in order to complete their journey.

As I began the ascent towards the main part of the bridge, I had a sudden sharp pain in my stomach and had to stop. Putting it down to a spot of cramp, I carried on and admired the scenery around me. The first part of the bridge was high above the marshland below and I could see small patches of land where locals were growing crops. Natural canals crisscrossed the area, making the vegetation lush and green.

Leaning over the guard rail, I waved to some of the workers a hundred feet below, shouting a greeting. They were clearing an area about the size of a tennis court, the foliage cut and pushed back, exposing a soily brown footprint ready for planting. To my left, I noticed a smart looking pavilion perched on a small ridgeline. It was obviously a viewing area for the bridge, probably for dignitaries.

Continuing on, after the ascent had flattened out, the pain in my stomach returned and I knew I was in trouble. There were no steps down to ground level, nowhere to go to the toilet and I had to pull down my trousers in a hurry and accept the inevitable. Thankfully I was out of sight of the guard post. I bowed my head and endured the shame as a man on a bicycle rode past, shaking his fist and giving me a stern look. He looked the sort who would tell the soldiers. Quite what they would do I wasn't sure and I apologised as best as I could.

Soon afterwards, some women came walking from the opposite direction and, looking away, I could hear them giggling and laughing at my predicament. I had really enjoyed my lunch, but now I was paying the price. I was truly glad that I hadn't had a second helping. I began to wonder what I would have found if I had visited the kitchen. I fled the scene of the crime before any soldiers or officials arrived. It wasn't quite the entrance to Zambezia Province, the final one on my journey, that I had imagined.

As I hit the main section of the bridge that passed over the river itself, I heard hippos and had to stop and look. There were about five of the beasts a few hundred metres away near a sand bar, enjoying the coolness of the water on a baking day. A young one was with its mother, who was watching the bank for any signs of danger. It was a wonderful sight.

Crossing to the far side of the bridge, I was now entering the final and one of the largest Provinces in the country. I found a path down to the water, disturbing a small herd of cows on the way, and washed myself by some dugouts, taking care to look for crocodiles. Spotting some fishermen under the bridge, I hid my embarrassment and finished washing before dressing quickly and retracing my steps.

Back in Tete, I had been told about a place called Cuacua Lodge this side of the river, used by expats and visiting fishermen, and I set out to find it in the hope of staying the night. It was still a few hours from sunset, but I felt I needed somewhere decent to sleep in my fragile state and didn't want

179

to walk until dark. I had about a hundred and forty kilometres left to reach the Indian Ocean and wanted to begin the final section in style.

Chapter Eleven - The Kindness of Strangers

I spotted a sign for the lodge and looked up to see the place on the hillside, nestled in trees. Following the rutted track for about a kilometre, I passed an empty guard hut and walked up the stone steps, admiring the level of workmanship that had gone into its construction. Flat stones of different colours, shades and sizes had been moulded together to create a grand entrance that wound up to the main building.

Arriving at the bar in a smart patio area, I noticed a couple of Mozambicans in chinos and polo shirts enjoying a beer in the shade. Apart from them, the place seemed deserted. I took my pack off, ordered a Coke from the barman and stood by the railings overlooking a green swimming pool. This was the kind of place I could stay for a while, I thought, considering my tiredness and dodgy stomach.

Looking down towards the pool, surrounded by a lounging area and neatly tended gardens, I could see the Zambezi in the distance, oblivious to time and those who relied on it. There too was the bridge I had just crossed, the metal arches a dull colour in the sun's dwindling rays. It was late afternoon and although I could and should have walked for a few more hours, I felt that I had earnt a rest in such a pleasant spot as this.

Trying my luck, I asked to see the manager and after a few minutes, an Indian looking man appeared and asked me in English what I wanted. I told him about my expedition and the places I had passed through, and explained that I had sought help on the way to aid my progress. With a big smile on my face, I asked him if he could offer such assistance, by giving me a room to rest in for the night. I told the man that I had been helped a number of times along the way. With a serious look, the manager informed me he would call the owner as he didn't have the authority to make such a decision, and disappeared back to his office. Back in Tete I had been informed that the owner was an expat and knew that the network was strong. I was somehow convinced that permission would be given, based on my experiences with expats in the country, and settled myself into one of the comfortable chairs to enjoy my drink.

A few minutes later, the man reappeared and judging by his dour look I knew that it wasn't to be my day. Explaining that the owner could not be contacted, he told me that I couldn't stay for free, but that he could offer a discount. The price he gave for one night brought water to my eyes and after thanking him, I made a speedy exit.

My idea hadn't gone to plan, but I was glad that I had at least tried. I now had to find somewhere to spend the night and after quickly checking my satnav, walked towards a settlement called Lago Chipancane a few kilometres away.

The villagers looked at me with amusement as I asked for the Mfumu and was shown to a little house close to the river. The elder appeared and I explained with sign language that I wanted permission to sleep in his yard. He nodded in understanding, but had someone take me to the house of his 'deputy' on the other side of the village.

While I waited for the deputy, his daughter brought me a chair and made some tea, making me feel welcome. Her father eventually arrived, smiled and shook my hand and with another man who spoke some English, we set off along a track out of the settlement. I asked where we were going a few times and the deputy just smiled at me and pointed into the distance.

After a few kilometres, we arrived at another village called Lago Nhacunca, presumably twinned with the settlement I had just passed through and was introduced to its head, a clean-cut man of middle age with a studious look. He was holding council in what looked like the village meeting room, a boalo, with a desk for himself and basic chairs lining the walls. It was a simple affair made of mud and wood, but it resonated with the authority of the discussions and decisions that were taken there. The deputy explained who I was and my new host nodded his head and signalled with his hand for me to take a seat. He seemed genuinely pleased to see me and through a teacher acting as interpreter, asked about my journey, particularly the section from Tete.

Cold Cokes and biscuits were brought and at that moment I realised that not being given permission to stay at Cuacua Lodge had been fortunate, as my journey experience was about to be enhanced. As we chatted, a man appeared at the door and gently clapped his hands. My host reciprocated and the new arrival began speaking, as if to pass on an important message. I had witnessed the behaviour in other villages, where the clapping was a signal to be allowed to speak.

Later, my host showed me where I could put up my tent in the grounds of the village school nearby and told me, by moving his fingers to his mouth, that food was being prepared. Thanking him, I established my camp and surveyed my surroundings as the murkiness of the evening descended. On three sides were scruffy single-storey buildings with peeling paint, some of the bricks crumbling and panes of glass missing from a few of the windows. As a place of learning it wasn't the grandest, but at least it was a place, when earlier in my trip I had seen pupils with far less.

Walking over to the hub of the village, I was amazed at how tidy it was. The bare earth of the main street was swept clean and there wasn't a piece of rubbish anywhere, unlike most of the other villages I had stayed in. The few shops were tidy and well maintained and I realised that it was all because of my host, who obviously demanded high standards. Nurturing an ice-cold beer at one of the shops, I watched the villagers wandering around in the gathering gloom.

Back at the agreed time, I found a plate of nshima and fish for me sitting on the desk. I still hadn't taken to nshima, after trying it several times, but I was hungry after the exertions of the day and enjoyed the meal, especially the spicy tomato sauce served with it. As I stood up after the meal, the teacher wrapped his hand around my arm to get my attention and spoke quietly.

'You need to be careful from now on, as you approach the sea.'

'Why is that?' I asked, surprised.

'The people in the delta are a little crazy!' he said, emphasising his point by tapping his fingers against his head.

'How crazy?'

'Ah, they are different from us. Very strange in their minds.'

The teacher explained to the village leader what he was telling me and the older man grunted and slowly shook his head.

'Just keep moving fast to the sea,' the teacher instructed, assuring me that I would be alright.

As I walked back to my lonely tent, I thought about the kindness of my hosts. These people were poor and led a simple existence, with a life expectancy of just fifty-five years I learnt later and yet they helped a weary traveller on the road without a second thought.

Sometime in the night, I woke to a full bladder and chastised myself for not going earlier. Strapping on my shoes, I stepped into the darkness wearing just boxer shorts and shirt and within seconds my legs were being attacked by mosquitoes. I knew I was close to the river and had spotted lagoons on the way to the village, a perfect habitat for the insects. I don't know how the locals put up with such an onslaught, but this was their home and they probably had little option to move elsewhere. I was relieved when I finally made it back into the tent but a number of mosquitoes had followed me inside and I spent the next ten minutes dispatching them.

As I drifted off back to sleep, I was reminded of the fate of Mary Moffat, the wife of David Livingstone who died at the age of forty-one on the opposite side of the river to where I now camped. On a return journey to the Zambezi with her husband, she had succumbed to malaria and been buried at the Catholic mission at Chupanga, under a large baobab tree and near the remains of two English naval officers who had died a few decades before. It was 1862, long before a cure for the disease had been found and the inscription on her gravestone is a simple one:

'Here repose the mortal remains of Mary Moffat, the beloved wife of Doctor Livingstone, in humble hope of a joyful resurrection by our saviour Jesus Christ.'

For several days, a guard was posted by the grave for protection until it was built up with bricks, apparently still in place today.

In happier times, David Livingstone had been much taken with the area and on his first visit wrote that:

'At Shupanga, a one-storied stone house stands on the prettiest site on the river. In front a sloping lawn, with a fine mango orchard at its southern end, leads down to the broad Zambesi, whose green islands repose on the sunny bosom of tranquil water'. (1)

Despite the mosquito bites and hard ground, I slept relatively well and emerging from my tent saw women ambling through the settlement, ready to start their day. They were carrying basic tools, machetes and hoes, and were no doubt on their way to inspect their crops and try to tame the bush. I was away from Lago Nhacunca by seven after thanking my host for his kindness and was pointed to the correct track to take from a choice of many. I had thirty-five kilometres to cover in the day to reach Mopeia, a logical step on the way to the ocean.

For the first few hours, the track was interesting and weaved up and down through date palm groves and copses of hardwood and I caught fleeting glimpses of the Zambezi in the distance. I met few people, but guessed that the locals were out farming or trying their luck on the river. Passing through tiny settlements, I would buy a warm bottle of Fizz and use the sugar to spur me on for the next section.

At one stop, a boy walked past me pulling his toy. It was a branch from a palm tree, where the wood had been smoothed out and a set of coconut shell wheels attached. He was manoeuvring the toy through the soil, turning sharply as he went and he had the biggest smile you could imagine. It always amazed me in Mozambique how people made things from virtually nothing.

In late morning, when the track had straightened out and begun to follow electricity cables and while I was sitting on my pack taking a welcome drink of water, some slight movement opposite caught my eye. I kept dead still, watching the sparse vegetation and slowly the head of a snake appeared at the edge of the track, some ten feet away.

Gradually, as more of the reptile appeared, I got a better look and guessed that it was a cobra. It was light brown in colour and perhaps six feet. I had heard that there were spitting cobras in Mozambique and was glad that my sunglasses were on. Often, when I took a break, I would take them off and hang them from my shirt, to wipe the dirt from my eyes and sweat from my face.

I watched the snake in fascination as it rapidly flicked its tongue to test the air, but when it started to move out further, I knew I had to do something. At a sudden movement from my arm, the creature changed course in the blink of an eye and slithered back into the scrub, disappearing in seconds.

I set off again, keeping a watchful eye on the undergrowth by the side of the track and made good progress. The Zambezi had long since disappeared as the route took me away from it and I looked forward to seeing it again as I closed in on the ocean. The path went up and down through the bush, which surprised me as I expected the terrain to flatten as I approached the delta.

The track hit a T-junction and the electric cables disappeared north. My compass told me to continue straight, but there was only thick vegetation with no clear way through. Consulting my satnav, the track I was on wasn't shown, so I headed south on a small path towards the river, hoping to get back on course. After an hour of following the path through semi-jungle, thankfully it joined a more substantial track in the direction I wanted.

I was pleased to see the telecoms mast of Mopeia later in

the afternoon. I walked past a large school as I entered the town, where teenage children looked at me in bewilderment. Few white people made it this far east along the Zambezi and I could hear the kids chatting excitedly to each other about my arrival.

The town had suffered violence the year before, like some of the places in bandit country that I had already passed through. Here, elements of the Renamo group had attacked the police station and other government buildings, causing injuries and even some fatalities. It seemed they were unable to give up their violent past in a country that had suffered enough. Later, I was to learn that the town was also in the unenviable position of having a virus named after it, which is carried in rats.

I hit the main road and turned towards the heart of the town, noticing the wide streets and orderly nature of the place. Spotting the police station straight away, I walked in, to the surprise of the policeman on duty, and asked if I could camp in the grounds.

After checking my passport and consulting with a senior colleague, permission was given and I was pointed to a spot across the road near a half-finished building. I assumed it was additional accommodation for the police, but it looked like the money had run out or there was a delay. All I could see was an empty two storey structure with building materials scattered around the courtyard, a partial corrugated iron fence surrounding it.

Thanking the officer, I walked up the main avenue, noticing a large tree next to an abandoned house, where bats were fighting with each other for the best hanging point. As a new arrival approached a branch, it disturbed those already in place and there was a flapping of wings and strange sounds as order was restored.

Looking around, Mopeia had probably been a smart provincial town in the Portuguese era, judging by the size and construction of the buildings, but most were now falling apart and overgrown. I walked past shops selling hardware and seeing a place that sold cold drinks I stepped inside, smiling when I noticed a line of fridges humming quietly away, watched by an Indian-looking man. I knew that Islam had taken root in the north of the country, following its control of the slave trade along the Zambezi and wondered if the man's ancestors had settled in the town.

Taking off my pack, I bought a can of beer and took a sip, relishing the taste as the liquid cooled my throat. As I was taking another drink, still in the shop, a black hand grabbed the can and pulled it violently away from me and I was pushed to one side.

Astonished, I turned and looked at the perpetrator, standing there cockily and drinking my beer. He was a local, aged about thirty and about my height, just under six foot tall. He was shirtless, but dressed in tattered old trousers and his eyes had a wild look.

In a flash of anger, I stepped towards him and he ran outside, the can still held in his hand. Once on the road, he slowed to a walk, not expecting me to follow and began to guzzle the cold liquid as fast as he could. Still shocked and furious in equal measure, I ran at him and rugby-tackled him to the ground, the can dropping to the floor. He was strong and agile and after a scuffle, where he elbowed me in the face, I managed to pin him down and forced his head into the dirt. I shouted a few choice words, something about getting between an Englishman and his beer, then pushed him away and watched him leave as other locals jeered and threw sticks at him, pointing the way out of town.

'What the hell was that all about?' I asked the shopkeeper when I returned, dusting myself down.

'Oh, he is well known to us and always causing problems here,' replied the man.

'So why don't you get the police involved?'

'They're not interested in the "crazy ones" as there is nowhere to send them.'

'Why don't they put him in the local jail for a bit to calm him down?' I asked.

'There's no point. He'll come out and steal again.'

'So, there's nothing the authorities can do?' I asked.

'Very little. We don't have mental institutions in Mozambique, so these kind of people just live in the community and cause trouble. Every town has them. Sometimes they are banished from where they live, but they never go far.'

Shaking my head, I bought another beer to replace what had been lost and went to sit in the shade outside to try to rationalise what had happened. I touched my eyebrow as it was a little sore and found some blood on my fingers. I noticed that a nail had also been partly torn off on one of my fingers, which was now throbbing with pain. Inspecting my trousers, I saw that I had an inch-long tear just below the knee, which also annoyed me as I wasn't carrying a needle and thread to fix it.

I had made it through most of the country with few problems and was enjoying the journey, but felt that it was starting to sour. Putting the incident behind me, I asked the shopkeeper if there was anywhere good to eat and he pointed down the street to a restaurant on the corner, saying it was his favourite place. The eatery, Girassol Kinho's, or Kinho's Sunflower, certainly looked the part, with a shaded seating area out front and freshly painted beige walls. I had a quick look in the kitchen before sitting down and decided to have some freshly made chips, as the meat in plastic buckets had seen better days. I didn't want to be ill again, as I had to get to the finishing point at Chinde and out again and knew I would need all my strength to do that. When the chips arrived, I covered them in lemon juice and salt, with some ketchup on the side, and left the place a happy man.

Returning to the police station, I gave a description of my assailant to the duty officer who smiled and shrugged his shoulders, telling me it was unfortunate. He asked if I wanted some of his men to try to find the man and I told him that I did. Smiling more broadly, he informed me there would be a charge to carry out the service. I declined and headed off disconsolately to my camping spot.

Later, when I was trying to get to sleep, I heard a man nearby, shouting in my direction. Initially I ignored him, hoping he would go away, but when he began to pace around my sanctuary and shake the tent, I felt I had to act.

'Speak to the Comandante!' I yelled out.

There were a few more shouts followed by murmurs and then it went quiet. I assumed it had been an over-zealous night watchman who hadn't been told of my arrival, but it jangled my nerves after a difficult day.

Chapter Twelve - A Change in Atmosphere

As I left Mopeia early the next morning, locals were gathering at a motorbike taxi station with their sacks of possessions, agreeing fares with the drivers. This form of transport was quite common in this part of the country, as there were few cars or minibuses. Crossing a bridge over lagoons and marshland in the early morning sunshine, I was determined to enjoy the day and put the experiences of Mopeia behind me.

After an hour, I reached a turnoff to the right, with a board announcing a new road next to the river. I was tempted to try it, but it didn't show on my satnav and I assumed it hadn't yet been finished. I asked some locals sauntering past about the route to Luabo, my next major waypoint about sixty kilometres away, and they told me to stay on the main road. When I pointed to the new route, they shook their heads vigorously, confirming that it wasn't finished.

I passed the small settlement of Mazaro that had probably not changed in a hundred years. Basic dwellings of mud and stick huts leant precariously to one side and one wondered if they would survive the next storm. David Livingstone had described the scenery that I was passing through with little enthusiasm and I had to agree with him:

'The scenery is tame and uninteresting. On either hand is a dreary uninhabited expanse, of the same level grassy plains, with merely a few trees to relieve the monotony'. (1)

I walked for hours without seeing another settlement and in parts the tarmac road was broken with numerous holes, then it reverted to soil and rock. Gradually, it began to veer towards the Zambezi, until at last I was next to it. In front of me were what looked like islands, five hundred metres away. The river was starting to widen as it approached the ocean. A fisherman in a dugout canoe was throwing his net hopefully in the water, no doubt trying to put something on the table.

In the early afternoon, as I passed some dwellings by the

side of the road, a man sitting in a chair with a beer bottle by his side called out to me. I had experienced many pseudo officials earlier in the journey, particularly drunken ones, asking for my papers and I was unwilling to comply. I shrugged my shoulders, increased my pace and carried on, hoping to get clear of the nuisance. There was a sound of a chair falling over and shouts, followed by rapid footsteps and I walked faster, without looking around.

After a few hundred metres, with the man continuing to shout, I glanced over my shoulder to see how far behind he was. What I saw gave me a shock. As well as the man, there were now about ten youths behind him, looking angry. I'm not sure where they came from, but they might have been resting in the shacks and woken by the drunken man.

'Shit!' I whispered under my breath, wondering why my presence was causing such anguish with the locals.

Increasing my stride, I kept moving along the track, hoping they'd get bored. After about a kilometre of fast walking and sensing that I was getting away from the group, I glanced over my shoulder again and saw that they had dropped back, but were still coming for me.

'Very strange,' I murmured frustratedly, as I concentrated on the road and continued.

I knew that I was fit after trekking for a month and could keep going for a long time, even carrying a light pack, but was concerned that my followers would keep at it and try to catch up. What my crime was I didn't know, probably not stopping when instructed to, but I felt that negotiations with the mob would not end well.

It was at about this time that I heard a truck behind me and moved to the side of the road to let it pass. It screeched to a halt next to me, the door was flung open and the passenger spoke firmly in English.

'You should get in, sir!' he urged.

Not giving it a second thought, I jumped in beside him and we roared away in a cloud of dust.

'Much obliged!' I said, looking in the mirror at the

diminishing figures. 'How did you know to stop?'

'We sometimes have trouble when the villagers block the road and demand money. Sometimes they beat drivers who do not pay!'

I thought back to sections of the road where I had seen logs and rocks by the side of the road, now realising what they were.

'And where are the police?'

'Ach, they don't like to leave the towns and cause trouble for the people here.'

I told my companions, the driver from Mozambique and the passenger from Malawi, about what had happened and they nodded, as if they had heard it all before. They were deliverymen, operating between Caia and Luabo, and dropped off supplies and building materials to settlements along the way. It was a relief to be in the truck, but I knew that I would have to jump out soon and somehow make up the lost kilometres when I walked around Chinde at the end of my journey.

After we had been driving for about ten minutes and were well clear of the pursuers, I asked the driver to pull over and after some discussion he did so. It was good that they were concerned about my welfare, but my journey had to be on foot. Waving them off, I continued towards Luabo, the river shimmering in the afternoon sun beside me.

The rest of the day passed without incident and I saw few people on the road. It had been troublingly eventful and an hour before sunset I began to look for a campsite well away from the track and human interference. Finding a spot close to the water and hidden by thick undergrowth, I erected my tent quickly and settled down to a cold supper, not wanting to risk a fire.

As I tried to sleep, I heard the ominous sound of mosquitoes buzzing close to my tent, even brushing the sides and trying to break in to my sanctuary. David Livingstone rarely used a tent on his expeditions and when he did, it was normally at one of his supply bases like Sena or Chupanga. Apparently, he preferred to lay his rug on a bed of grass next to his companions and somehow managed to sleep, despite the attentions of insects. It was no wonder that the majority of his expedition caught malaria, with some succumbing to the disease, and I was glad I had taken all necessary precautions to prevent illness.

I was away early the following morning and already strolling along the track well before the sun made an appearance. The aggression shown by villagers the day before was preying on my mind and not wanting a similar experience, I had decided to stop at Luabo, about thirty kilometres away. It was the last settlement before the ocean and I could rest up there, hopefully find a restaurant and perhaps find somewhere to stay.

The track followed the course of the river and every so often I would scramble down to the water's edge, check for crocodiles and dunk my cap into the water in order to keep my head cool. The liquid would wet my hair and run down my shirt and although only a temporary solution to tackle the heat, it was worth it every time.

On the Zambezi, near Luabo

A few hours later, I came across the perfect drinks stall, facing the river. It was slightly larger than one of those old red telephone boxes that can still be seen in parts of Britain. Inside were soft drinks and biscuits stacked to the ceiling and the proprietor had put up a grass canopy for shade and dragged in some logs to sit on. With bottle of fizzy drink in hand, I wandered over to the river's edge and watched my old friend flow quietly past. Birds were skimming the water, hunting for insects, and further upstream a hippo was grunting, the sound carrying clearly through the air. It was a fabulous spot and I was reluctant to leave it.

The masts in the distance signalled that I was close to Luabo and I was looking forward to spending time out of the sun. The track alongside the river had been interesting, but with no trees lining the route, there had been no shade and I was wilting like a flower without water. As I approached, there was a row of old buildings on my right and what looked like an overgrown football field opposite.

Passing a line of motorbike taxis, I turned into the heart of the town along a litter-strewn street with stray dogs looking for scraps. It was a scruffy place and I was surprised that the locals hadn't tried to clean it up. I found a shop selling cold drinks and buying one, looked for somewhere to take the weight off my feet.

Locals initially eyed me with curiosity, but soon got bored and moved off to go about their business. There was a bustling market opposite with 'Mercado' written into the brick of a decaying arch, and I found a place to sit. Women were coming and going to buy their supplies and then walking home with wicker baskets atop their heads.

After I had spent half an hour relaxing out of the sun, a man in his twenties with smart casual clothes wandered over and opened his phone shop next to me.

'Where have you come from?' he asked in English, as he unlocked the shutters on the window.

'Zumbo' I replied 'and heading for Chinde.'

'That is too far!' he smiled.

'Yes, but it has been an interesting journey!'

'You must have seen many things?'

'I have, but not all of them good,' I told him, recounting events from the days before.

'We have some bad people in this area, so you must take care.'

He entered his shop and locals began to arrive to buy phone cards. After a while, when business had died down, he came to sit next to me and told me of his plans. The year before, he had set up a small shop around the corner selling clothes and had done well. Moving into the main street to sell phones, accessories and small electrical goods, his fortunes had really taken off. Before, there had been no such shop and he had benefited from people's desire to communicate with others. He told me that even though the people were poor, they could always find money for phones. The young man had an energy about him and I was glad he was making the most of his opportunities.

He asked if I was hungry and not having eaten anything hot since Mopeia, I told him that I was. I had actually eaten little in previous days and craved some hot, nourishing food. Taking out his phone, he began to call a few places and after a few minutes, told me he had found somewhere.

'I will take you to the place,' he informed me.

'What do they cook?' I asked, amazed with his help.

'Oh, anything. Chicken, fish, rice, potatoes…'

'Sounds great!' I grinned. 'How far is it?'

'Not so far. Let's go!' and locking up his shop, he led me through town to the restaurant a few minutes away.

It was a pleasant, clean-looking place, with chequered plastic tablecloths, table tidies and a waft of freshly cooked food. I asked my companion if the food was good and he nodded, telling me that he ate there all the time. He probably had a stake in the business, judging by his entrepreneurial flair, but I didn't mind as he had taken the trouble to help. Ordering some chicken and rice for me, he gave me his phone number in case I needed any help in the future and disappeared back into town.

Leaving the restaurant an hour later, I rejoined the main road and headed south. The food had been well cooked and plentiful and I was pleased to see the cleanliness of the kitchen when I paid for the meal. The owner obviously took food hygiene seriously, unlike others I had witnessed on the road, who had viewed it as optional.

I passed decaying grand old buildings set back from the road, knowing that this had once been a successful, bustling town during the rule of the Portuguese. It had been a centre for the production and processing of sugar cane, which had been exported up and down the East African coast, but the industry was no more as the locals now only grew a few crops close to the river.

A large, whitewashed, well-kept church with a bell tower at one end stood surrounded by a neatly trimmed hedge, and I was glad that at least one building in the town was cared for. Walking through Zambia on the way to Mozambique, I had seen a multitude of churches, often small, in almost every village and of every denomination. In Mozambique I had seen few churches on my journey along the Zambezi except in the towns, and those I had seen had almost certainly been built in the Portuguese era. It seemed that few new churches were being built, although so many religious charities poured money into Africa. The graveyard in front of this church looked crumbling and overgrown and I strolled over to inspect some of the headstones. Some were ornate and expensive-looking and I wondered about the lives of the Europeans who had settled there and would die before their time.

David Livingstone had referred to the river delta area as 'the white man's grave' due to the prevalence of disease as well as unruly tribes. Malaria has been the cause of many deaths in the Zambezi delta, then and now, and it was sad to think of the early settlers who had travelled all the way from their home country with such promise, only to be cut down in their prime. Moving deeper into the graveyard, I noticed smaller, plainer gravestones clustered together, possibly for the locals who had succumbed to the same fate as their visitors.

Further on, I spotted a large one-storey building set back from the road, with vegetation climbing up the sides. It resembled a castle with towers on each corner and a thick wooden door in the centre. It looked sinister and strange and peering closer, I saw chunky bars on the windows and realised it was the former jail. It was obviously built by the Portuguese to punish the locals, for what crimes I was not sure, but the unfortunates incarcerated there would have no doubt had a bad time. The Portuguese, whilst developing the country for their own ends, treated the indigenous population badly and this rotting jail was another symbol of their tenure.

On his expedition, David Lemon had also passed through the town and his observations were less than positive:

'There was no piped water and electricity depended on the reliability of diesel supplies. Luabo was not a tiny forest village but a major river port and had once been a thriving town. Now it was a desiccated husk of what once had been and my heart ached for the ordinary people of this country.' (3)

I had been told the police station was at the southern end of town, but had trouble finding it and asked a passer-by for directions. He pointed along the road out of town and I set off again looking left and right. Just as I was leaving Luabo, I spotted a derelict building on my left with police officers relaxing in the shade. I waved to them and an officer with a stripe on his arm pushed himself out of his chair and ambled over to find out what I wanted. I asked if I could put up my tent nearby and he led me to an old building with a red tiled roof on the other side of the road, where a desk sat in the entrance. An officer who could speak some English was called, and asked me why I was there and where I was going. I recounted the story of my journey, which he relayed to his superior, who was slowly leafing through my passport.

'You have come from Zumbo?' the junior man asked, astounded.

'I have,' I told him, telling him of the places I had visited on route.

I explained that I had walked along the north shore of Lake Cahora Bassa, something which hadn't been done since David Livingstone was there in the 1850s.

'Very far!' he said shaking his head. 'You must be very strong!'

'Perhaps. I have a light pack so I can walk quickly.'

I asked if they knew of Dr Livingstone, the famous explorer and he told me he did and that his journeys along the Zambezi were taught in school. As we were chatting, more officers entered the room and listened to the story. Some chuckled at what they were hearing, whilst others just looked on, studying me with interest.

After further discussion, I asked again if I could stay and the senior man nodded, smiled and gave his consent. I was shown to a patch of land behind the building and hastily erected my tent on the bare earth.

Walking up a bank, I admired the view as the Zambezi River flowed closely past me and noticed the vegetable patches neatly laid out in squares. Beans, squash and cabbages seemed to be the order of the day, growing in what looked like extremely fertile soil. A basic, unpainted wooden craft, with a spluttering engine and a few tolerant passengers on board, was following the near shore and my friendly waves caused little reaction.

Looking along the river bank, I noticed a multitude of birds which I hadn't seen for the last few days and enjoyed watching them fly across the water as they began to look for somewhere to roost. Some smaller birds pecked at morsels on the ground whilst others, like the herons, scanned the shore for unsuspecting minnows. David Livingstone, someone who missed little on his travels, also observed the birds in this part of Mozambique where I was currently standing:

'The marshes support prodigious numbers of many kinds of water-fowl. Near the edge, and on the branches of some favourite tree, rest scores of plotuses and cormorants, which stretch their snake-like necks, and in mute amazement turn one eye and then another towards the approaching monster [Livingstone's boat]. ' (1)

It was approaching sunset. Feeling some refreshment was in order, I gave some money to one of the junior policemen to fetch in drinks for my hosts. One of his colleagues set out chairs on the grass and we chatted for a few hours about my journey and life in the town. They were amazed that I could carry everything I needed in such a small pack and I reminded them that in a hot country, you didn't need much gear.

The men reflected on their time in Luabo, telling me they didn't like the town because it was so remote. Like other policemen I had met on the journey, they had all been posted in from around Mozambique, far from their families and loved ones. For most, it would take a few days to get home due to the poor infrastructure and transportation links in the country.

I asked about the threat of malaria and they became serious, despite the influence of the beer. Some had contracted the disease and ended up in the local clinic; all expected to get it at some point. I had taken anti-malarial pills for much of my time in Zambia and Mozambique and had been careful with using bug sprays and a net in my tent. The young officers sitting around me had no pills or sprays and few apparently had nets to protect themselves against mosquito bites in the night. I felt sad for them, posted miles away from home in a swampy river delta that offered little relief.

As if on cue, the mosquitoes began to build and despite liberal use of bug spray, I was bitten on the neck. Swiping at the irritant, I caught the insect and studied it in my hand. Mosquitoes in the Zambezi delta seemed to be twice the size of other mosquitoes and I wondered if they were a super subspecies. I bid my hosts goodnight and hastily retreated to the safety of my tent.

The road out of Luabo followed close to the river and I

passed by the decaying, giant sugar-cane processing plant. It was a huge tangled mess of rusting metal and rotten concrete and I tried to imagine it in its former glory. Once, it had produced thousands of tons of sugar every year and employed workers from near and far, but now it was being reclaimed by the undergrowth. I found it surprising that no businessmen had rekindled the industry in what was obviously a highly productive area, but it was the same story in other parts of Africa as well. Often, when the colonialists moved out, the country would fall to pieces and start to go backwards, as I had seen for myself in other parts of the continent.

On his travels through the area, David Livingstone noticed the quality of the natural resources for farming:

'The soil is wonderfully rich, and the gardens are really excellent. Rice is cultivated largely; sweet potatoes, pumpkins, tomatoes, cabbages, onions, peas, a little cotton, and sugar-cane are so raised.' (1)

I had thirty kilometres to walk to a spot on the river bank where I could catch a boat to Chinde Island. I would then walk the final twenty-kilometre section to the town of Chinde itself, where the journey would end. I was in high spirits to finish the trek and was looking forward to going home, despite some great experiences along the way. The rutted track kept straight and true and began to head inland, as the river curled away. Few locals were walking on the route and those that I saw would often scuttle off into the bushes and disappear.

Passing through the tiny settlement of Bento a few hours later, I took a moment to rest by a shack that sold drinks. Small children began to appear and after a few minutes I had quite an audience. A man, probably in his thirties, wandered up to me and demanded in broken English that I buy him some gin.

'Why's that?' I asked, heaving a sigh.

'You have money,' my new friend replied, not interested in me or my journey, but just what I had.

201

I gave the man half an unfinished pack of biscuits I had been eating and he walked off with them behind the shack, without thanking me. Swinging on my pack, I left the place to be on my own again and continued walking as the heat began to build.

The track began to veer back towards the Zambezi until it was parallel with the river again and I dropped down to a small beach to take some water. Pushing my bottle under the surface filled it within seconds and I withdrew my hand quickly and climbed the bank. The policemen in Luabo had told me about crocodile attacks along their section of the river, normally when locals were taking water or washing their clothes, and I didn't want to appear on their fatality lists.

The vegetation on either side of me was tall and lush, and I continued to see small farming plots hacked out of the bush, where locals were growing their own vegetables. I also noticed the high number of gravestones next to the river, some tended and others overgrown. Some markers were made of wood, others of rough stone, and all had been created with care, unlike other gravestones I had seen on route. I hadn't seen a chapel since Luabo and guessed that the people buried their loved ones close to home, rather than taking them to the town.

An hour later, I was walking at a good pace and just as I was passing some kind of workers' camp, the track swung towards the river and stopped. In front of me were a few small shops and further on, a muddy beach with some basic craft tied to the shore. I had expected the mooring to be further east and, checking my satnav, estimated that it should have been about ten kilometres away. The old location must have been abandoned for some reason and a new one established where I was standing. Walking down to the boats, I asked some men sitting on a bank when the next departure for Chinde Island was. They pointed to one of the boats and held up three fingers. I had a few hours to wait, so wandered back to a shop, bought a drink and some biscuits and took refuge under an awning.

Looking around, I realised that this really was the end of the line. I could go no further on this side of the Zambezi, as there was no path to follow and it wasn't an option to hack through the undergrowth and try to cross further down. Even if I did make it further down the river, it was unlikely that the infrequent boats would pull over and collect me. The mooring where I was now sitting had been selected for a reason and I had to use it to cross to the island.

As I was enjoying my lunch and savouring the view, some fellow travellers trundled past and made their way towards the boats. Soon after, as I was taking another swig of warm fizzy drink, a young man jogged over to me and urgently beckoned me towards the river.

'But it's only two o'clock!' I said. 'I thought it was leaving at three.'

The man looked over his shoulder and urged me on. Stepping through the mud towards one of the boats, the colour of English mustard, I noticed that it was filling up fast. Women were pushing bags over their heads into the vessel, whilst men helped others on board, lifting children and swinging them up. Painted on the front of it was the Portuguese name 'Mussagy'.

Heaving my pack up a makeshift ladder, I climbed through a gap in the rails and found a seat to the side. My transport looked safe enough though old and well used, unchanged in decades. It was about forty foot long by ten foot wide and the plank seats were arranged across the sharp angled hull of the vessel. The wooden roof was secured on a frame, providing shade from the sun. My fellow passengers, about twenty in total, with their bundles of belongings and boxes of food, watched me closely, no doubt wondering what I was doing there. As we were partly beached on the mud, some men sitting on the bank sprang into action and began to push the craft into deeper water.

Finally, we were off as the engine spluttered into life and we headed down the river. I looked across at the riverbank which was thick with vegetation and realised that I wouldn't have stood a chance trying to hack my way through it. As we glided over the mud-coloured water, the realisation that I was nearly at the end of my journey struck home. I felt satisfied to have covered the distance in an area where few white people ventured.

After twenty minutes, I spotted some huts in the distance and we chugged our way towards them. Soon, the bow of our boat nudged into the bank with a thud and the passengers grabbed their possessions and without ceremony, scrambled over the beams before stepping onto the mud. I had arrived on Chinde Island. On his journey, David Lemon's boat had bypassed this mooring and puttered directly on to Chinde town, thus negating the need to walk the final section.

The craft used to carry me across the
Zambezi to Chinde island

The basic huts I had seen belonged to fishermen, who were untangling their nets and cleaning the fish from the morning's catch. I half thought about pitching my tent nearby, as I wasn't going to reach Chinde before sunset. However, there was no food or drink to buy, so I followed the rest of the passengers onto a path away from the river.

After an hour, as I approached a village, a man in a yellow T-shirt raced out of his simple dwelling towards me and began to babble in Portuguese next to my shoulder. I politely listened to him for a few minutes and once he paused for breath, told him apologetically that I only spoke English and increased my stride. Ignoring my hint, he continued to talk and began to wave his hands. I wondered if he was one of those self-appointed officials who thought it their responsibility to check the papers of strangers passing through. He hadn't mentioned 'documento' or 'passport', so I wasn't sure what his gripe actually was.

Looking towards the village, it seemed a great spot to take a break. Tall palm trees swayed in the gentle breeze and little wooden houses lined the sandy track. Children were playing football on a grass field to my right and a few grownups, standing on the sidelines, were urging them on. There were no electric cables to be seen, which didn't surprise me in such a remote spot, but I felt for the locals who were unable to tap into such a necessary resource.

Ten minutes later, with the man still babbling at me, I stopped and turned to him, pointing back towards his house and urged him to go home. He just looked at me with a hurt look on his face and stayed where he was. Turning, I walked off towards the centre of the village, but a few minutes later I heard him talking behind me again. I found a shop and bought a bottle of warm pop, asking the owner if there was anywhere to buy hot food. Shaking his head dismissively, he wandered away as I looked for somewhere to rest.

The man in the yellow T-shirt came over again and started talking earnestly to me. Shaking my head, I pointed in the direction of his house again and he soon disappeared. Even though my drink was warm, it was still refreshing and I appreciated and savoured every drop.

According to my satnav, I had about fifteen kilometres to go and I began to think about where I might stay. There were unlikely to be any police stations, so I reconciled myself to staying in a village or finding a quiet spot out of view.

Setting off again, I looked for suitable campsites in the small settlements I passed through, but nothing appealed and I decided to push on towards Chinde town. I was now on a sparsely populated island, about the size and shape of the Isle of Wight, with the sea ahead and the river on either side. The Marromeu National Reserve was just a few kilometres south, home to lions, leopards and hyenas, as well as water buffalo the size of a car. It was not the time to stray off course.

At around five o'clock, coming to some huts by the side of the track, I asked people if I could put up my tent but was met with laughter and shooed away, as if I was an unwelcome vagrant. I was surprised, as so many locals on my journey had helped me, but these folk were different and I began to feel uneasy. Gone were the smiles and waves, to be replaced by stern looks and slow wagging fingers.

I walked on and arrived at a village, where a multitude of children aged from six to sixteen were playing football on a makeshift pitch. It was strange: there was no laughing or shouting, noises you would normally associate with football. There was no emotion.

Sitting down on my pack, I spotted a flat area at the end of the pitch that might make a camp site. By this time, the children had lost interest in the game and gathered closely around me, talking nervously to each other. Even though they were only children, there was something intimidating about their presence, particularly as there were no happy faces or laughter. Some women had also arrived and watched me suspiciously from the rear, faces stern and eyes unblinking.

Giving the signal for sleep and pointing to my preferred spot, I asked if I could stay and a teenage boy stepped forward saying, 'Mfumu'. Pulling on my pack, I followed the lad to find the man in charge. Glancing over my shoulder, I noticed that the crowd of about thirty kids was following us. We walked through the village and, stopping at the edge, I asked my guide how far it was to the leader's house. The boy signalled with his hands that it was far and I realised that the elder probably looked after a number of settlements.

'Don't worry, I'll just continue walking,' I indicated to the boy, thanking him for his help, not keen to stay with such miserable hosts.

He threw me a questioning look and shouted something back to his friends, who shot me angry glances. I tried to explain that I had changed my mind and strolled off as sunset approached.

I had been walking for about five minutes along the sandy track, admiring the trees and birds flying overhead, when a shiver went down my spine and I felt that something just wasn't right. Glancing over my shoulder, I saw the crowd of children walking towards me, about a hundred metres away. I noticed that some had picked up sticks, which they were carrying down by their sides.

'What the hell!' I whispered to myself as I increased my stride, wondering what I had done.

After another kilometre the crowd was still there, sending me the occasional whistle and jeer, although further away now. I increased my pace to get away from them for good. A little later, as I passed over a mound, I noticed that they were gone and breathed a sigh of relief. They had followed me for over two kilometres and I realised that something was seriously wrong in the delta. I wondered if inbreeding was the cause, due to the inaccessibility of the island. By not going to see the Mfumu and insisting on continuing on my own, I had probably broken some taboo, but the reaction of the teenagers concerned me.

As the light began to fade, the track passed through a large marshy area and I was attacked by mosquitoes, biting at my hands and face, and quickly applied repellent. The insects reduced their onslaught, but I continued to feel the occasional bite when one broke through my defences.

I checked my satnav and saw that I was still twelve kilometres from Chinde and pushed on, hoping to find somewhere to camp. When the track left the swamp, it swung sharply to the left and into trees and it felt like I was on the home straight. In places, the track became deep sand and difficult to walk through and I wondered how vehicles made it around the island without getting stuck.

Passing cooking fires, I thought about approaching one of the homes to ask if I could camp, but knew a white face might give someone a fright. Leaving the huts behind me, I took out my torch to inspect the ground, looking for suitable camping spots, and found small farm plots with rows of what looked like beans and cabbages. Near a pond, the mosquitoes returned with a vengeance and swarmed around my face.

Soon afterwards, the heavens opened and it began to rain. It was still the dry season and this was the first rain I had experienced on the trip. To travel light, I hadn't brought a waterproof jacket and my shirt began to soak in the deluge. I searched desperately for somewhere to camp, my torch flitting to either side of the track.

Eventually, after fifteen minutes in the torrential downpour, my light illuminated a patch of ground without any crops on it and I headed for it. Undoing my pack and continuing to be bitten and rained on, I quickly erected my tent and slid inside, relieved to rest. I was soaking wet and tired but pleased to be out of the storm and in a semblance of shelter. I had checked the ground thoroughly and knew that I wasn't camping on someone's vegetables, but I felt uneasy about the place from my earlier experience and planned to get away early the following morning.

I should have kept going.

Chapter Thirteen - Darkness

The night seemed to last forever and I got little sleep. My tent was pounded by gusting wind and rain and when it eased off, the mosquitoes returned and buzzed around the net, desperately trying to get in. I awoke at six, my body cramped, cold and aching, and I pulled on my shoes. It was quiet outside and I was hoping that I could slip away to Chinde before it was fully light.

Glancing quickly at my satnav, it showed that I was just outside the settlement of Chimuaza and had about eight kilometres to go. As I was keen to get to the town and complete my journey, I estimated that it would take me just over an hour and a half.

Unzipping the tent, I peered outside and was surprised to see some women on the track that I had been on the previous evening.

'Bom dia!' I shouted cheerily and waving my hand.

The women looked at me stony-faced and kept perfectly still and silent.

'Nice to see you too,' I said under my breath, as I began to dismantle my tent.

I was packed up in minutes, and as I was taking a drink of water, an older man appeared and walked up to me. He began speaking in an agitated tone, his finger pointing accusingly at my chest. I presumed he was asking what I was doing there and I gestured with my fingers in a walking motion that I was heading for Chinde. Not happy with my answers, he began shouting at me and looking around, as if he was expecting someone. I assumed that he was unhappy about where I had camped, but I pointed to the spot, trying to explain that it was obviously waste ground. Even without full daylight, it was clear to see that it was a scrubby area, without a crop to be seen.

I explained again to the man that I was heading for Chinde. He shook his head firmly and reached for my arm.

Brushing him off, I heard him shouting behind me and I walked quickly towards the track, wanting to get away. By now, a small crowd of about twenty people had gathered, eying me suspiciously and I noticed others approaching from behind. Offering another greeting and smiling broadly, I tried to lighten the mood and began to walk away.

Suddenly, there was a guttural shout and I heard footsteps racing towards me. I turned quickly to confront the danger. Standing in front of me was a tall local man with raggy clothes and a distinctive egg-sized lump on the edge of his forehead. He glared at me with flared nostrils and breathing hard, his anger palpable, and I calmly asked what I had done. At that moment, I noticed a few other men circle around me, cutting off my route to the town and knew that I had to somehow talk my way out of the situation. I asked again of the brute in front what I had done and he lunged for my pack, almost afraid of getting too close. Getting hold of a shoulder strap, he yanked it continually and we had a tug of war for a few moments. I hadn't had time to do up the waist strap due to my hurried departure and we were now in a serious tussle. Everything I had for the journey was in that pack and I wasn't going to give it up without a fight. Lashing out with my feet, I made the man step back but he kept a tight grip on the strap.

Suddenly, some men rushed forward and jumped on me from behind and I was forced to the floor, mud and sand covering my face. I tried to elbow one of the attackers who was sitting astride me, but he caught my arm and pushed the hand up my back, causing me to cry out in pain. He kept pushing it upwards and I thought for a moment he was trying to break it. I tried to wriggle to reduce the pressure.

'Tourist! I'm a tourist!' I cried out, not believing what was happening.

My words had no effect, as the weight of the man on top of me forced me into the dirt. I let out a few angry words and tried to slip out of their grasp, but it was no good. I wasn't going anywhere.

The first punch caught me in the side of the face, just

below the cheek bone. I had been expecting to be hit, but it shocked me all the same. It was a punch delivered with force, with meaning, and further blows followed, all to the head. Some sharp kicks then hit me in the sides, causing me to wince in pain.

'Behave yourselves!' I shouted, more out of annoyance than fear, but I knew the situation was getting way out of control.

I would have tried to block the blows, except they had now bound my hands tightly behind me with twine. My feet had also been tied tightly together with my belt and there was little I could offer in resistance. Someone rifled in my thigh pockets and I felt my phone being removed. A few more punches were thrown and my head rocked from side to side with the impact. I could taste blood in my mouth and wondered if they had dislodged a tooth.

'I'm a tourist! A tourist!' I shouted, but my pleas were met with further blows.

My head was spinning as I tried to understand what was happening and how a conversation had escalated so quickly. Pressed to the ground, I quickly took in the multitude of legs in my line of sight and wondered where everyone had appeared from.

I knew that I had only one card to play.

'Is the Mfumu here?' I asked anxiously of those nearest me.

I knew that everyone who could hear me knew what that meant, but my question was met with indifference. I asked again, more pressing and louder this time and my heart sank as no one stepped forward to help. My audience began to chatter and animated shouts pierced my brain as ideas as to what to do with me competed and echoed around the clearing, increasing in tempo.

I felt two hands grab my head and pull it violently to the back and then to each side. It was then jerked so hard upwards that I thought the intention was to remove it from my body altogether and I prayed that no long-term damage was being caused. Shouting out in pain and anger again, I wondered what I had done to be treated so badly. Surely, sleeping on some waste ground wasn't a capital crime?

'Where's the Mfumu?' I shouted again, but the shouts from the crowd only became louder.

I was then grabbed by my arms on both sides and dragged along the track in the direction away from Chinde. I glimpsed some huts in the distance and wondered where they were taking me. Small children and teenagers began laughing and shouting on either side as if this was some game and their taunts made me uneasy. One by one my shoes slipped off my feet and I could feel my socks scraping through the sandy soil.

After a few hundred metres, the man on my right, who was weaker than his friend, let go of my arm and his companion jerked me forward in frustration with renewed vigour. Seeing the opportunity, a woman who had been shouting at me from the sidelines rushed forward and grabbed the vacated limb with relish and pulled me along. As my new captor rubbed up against me, I caught a whiff of her scent and I almost gagged. The smell was of sweat, human waste, dirt and decay and it frightened me. At times, when our progress slackened, she gripped my arm ever tighter, bruising the muscle and as if possessed by demons, forcing us forward.

'Tourist! Tourist!' I shouted as we continued on our journey, but the villagers had already decided who I was and what was to come.

Eventually, in what seemed an eternity, we moved off the path towards more huts and into what looked like the centre of the settlement. In a snatched glance, I saw that the dwellings were basic with simple grass thatch roofs. The ground in front was flattened down and I could see a large mound of ash denoting a fire straight in front of me. I was forced onto my knees.

The children, who had quietened coming into the settlement, found their voice again and began jeering and shouting in earnest along with the adults. The crowd, old and young and close to a hundred people by now, formed a circle around me, the closest an arm's length away. I flexed my arm muscles behind me, trying to alleviate the soreness of being dragged.

A frightening thought rushed through my head. Was this what early missionaries to Africa experienced when they had failed to convert the flock and instead invoked their anger? Were these their final minutes of life before being dispatched with a heavy club and sent to meet their maker earlier than they had planned?

A man strode through the throng, over to the mound of ash, scooped up a handful and walked purposefully back towards me, his eyes never leaving my own. Depositing the ash onto my head, he rubbed it vigorously into my hair and I could feel the powdery matter falling down my unshaven face, getting into my eyes.

'Mfumu! Mfumu!' I shouted again, wanting the village leader to appear, calm everything down, make the nightmare disappear and allow me to complete my journey.

But all I saw was a sea of dark faces, shouting, jeering and hostile. I flexed my throbbing fingers behind me which had been stamped on during the scuffle.

The crowd pressed closer and I was hit hard with a fist in the back of the head several times. Then, a man, probably in his thirties, grabbed my arm, shouted in defiance at the crowd and with the assistance of someone else, pulled me roughly to another spot. The people, following closely behind, were not happy with his move and told him so through more shouts and cries, but he merely shouted back at them, pushing them away from me.

A few of the women began pointing their fingers at me and yelling hysterically at the top of their voices. They were more hostile than the men and I tried to work out why there was so much hatred, but my mind couldn't help me. It was as if I had stumbled into some centuries-old African ritual, only this was real and it was terrifying.

An old plastic chair was brought and I was pushed down into the seat. My hands and feet were still bound, but it was good to sit and take the strain off my knees, even if I was still getting sporadic punches to the back of the head.

A woman pushed through the mob and tapped the arm of one of the older men standing in front of me. In her hands was an iron, one of those heavy, old cast iron affairs that you still see in industrial era museums. The man glanced down at her, paused for a moment and slowly shook his head, before she reluctantly withdrew. The implement she was carrying was clearly meant to do me harm and my mind raced with the terrible possibilities.

A young man appeared out of the crowd and, speaking in broken English, told me he was a teacher. Asking why I was there, I quickly explained that I was heading for Chinde. He requested to see my papers and I told him they were in my pack, which I hadn't seen since being jumped on. The man looked around nervously, as the crowd continued to send shouts and insults my way, and I asked him to fetch the police as a matter of urgency.

'It is very bad what they are doing, but it is out of my hands. They will do what they need to do,' he replied hopelessly, glancing away from me.

I asked him as calmly as I could what the problem was and why I had been so badly mistreated.

The man paused before answering, staring into my eyes.

'They think you are a vampire!' he replied.

'For God's sake, I'm a trekker, a tourist, just passing through to Chinde!' I pleaded. 'Tell them!'

The man yelled to the crowd, translating what I had said, but was met with angry shouts in response.

'They are very angry with you being here and say you need to be punished.'

'Punished for what? I took shelter here because of the storm and mean these people no harm!'

'I will tell them, but they will not believe me,' the teacher replied, relaying my words.

I urged him again to call the police and he wandered away slowly out of my vision. More blows hit the back of my head forcing my face down and I was expecting something more substantial at any moment. As I looked up again, two older men stepped into the circle and began to push the crowd back, shouting as they did so. They were met with cries and hysterical screams, as the people protested.

More blows landed on my head and one of the older men chastised the puncher, signalling him away. I heard shouts from my right and saw a woman at the edge of the mob pointing at me wildly, eyes wide, baring her teeth. One of my protectors tried to calm her down but other females next to her joined in, some making hideous sounds. Every so often, the crowd would surge forward and I would be struck again and the elders would try to push them back, shouting in annoyance and trying to regain control. Once, I felt someone take a tuft of my hair and pull it sharply, forcing my head backwards. The nimble fingers, possibly those of a child, rubbed the hair between their fingers whilst continuing to pull, trying to gauge what it was.

It went on for what seemed like forever, with the crowd moving closer to me and then being pushed back. By now, the elders holding the line had acquired sticks which they were thrashing at the human surge, trying to force it back. It was if the horde was a living creature, with one brain and a multitude of limbs operating under its direction.

Finally, with relief, I spotted the top of what looked like a police truck arriving behind my tormentors and the mood gradually quietened. A man in plain clothes with a pistol slung across his chest moved cautiously through the crowd, followed by a few other officers carrying AK-47s, nervously looking left and right. The mob stepped back a few paces in silence and I could sense their frustration and anger at the arrival. When the man reached the open area in front of me, he asked a few questions of the elders. Grunting at the replies, he looked down at me before slowly casting his eyes around the village.

A large, heavily built policeman was directed over to me and pulled me out of the chair. Expecting him to cut my ties, I was surprised when he slapped metal handcuffs on and then gripped my shoulder. The teacher was called over and the senior officer asked him to relay some questions to me: What was I doing there? Where was I going? Did I have documents?

I provided responses to all of the questions and the officer signalled for me to be taken to the truck. As I was about to be pulled away, I asked the teacher to find my pack and shoes and hurried murmurs went around the crowd. The pack emerged a few minutes later, followed by the shoes and one of the officers carried them to the vehicle. I was to find out later that some belongings in the top pocket of the daysack, including a torch and sunglasses, had been stolen.

'Where's my phone?' I asked the teacher, who questioned the crowd.

It had photos I had taken along the journey, as well as useful contacts I might need on the way out of the country. It was also my property. After a few minutes, the brute with the bulging forehead stepped forward out of the crowd, stopped in front of me and glared into my eyes. Slowly, he slid the phone out of his shirt pocket and handed it to the teacher without emotion, who pushed it into one of my thigh pockets.

With my feet still bound, I was carried back to the truck and lifted into the open top rear, as the crowd silently watched me. Looking around to see if there was any sign of remorse, I saw none, only blank and hostile stares from figures as still as gravestones.

As we drove away, I smiled weakly at my audience and nodded my head, letting them know I wasn't beaten, as I tried to rationalise what had just happened. Driving rapidly to Chinde along the sandy track, I received curious glances from those walking alongside, who were probably wondering what was going on. Apart from the policemen sitting next to me, there were the two elders who had tried to push back the crowd, presumably coming along to provide a statement. As we bounced along, I began to try to make sense of what had just happened and realised that it must have been a ceremony of some kind, some precursor to what was to come.

Eventually, I spotted a tall communications tower in the distance, indicating that we were close to Chinde and the end of my journey. Passing decaying old mansions and run-down homes, we stopped at the main police station near a square. My cuffs and foot restraint were removed and I was bustled inside. The plain clothes officer turned out to be the Comandante and he headed for a chair behind a large wooden desk.

Another teacher was called to translate, and I was asked to explain myself once more. Describing my journey and the places I had passed through, the man interpreted my explanation to the officer, who looked at me with indifference. I asked the teacher why I had been attacked and he told me that it was an underdeveloped area and that people were very suspicious of outsiders. He explained that the villagers had been frightened by my arrival, thought I had been there to steal their blood and were planning to kill me.

The thought of receiving 'village justice' at the hands of the mob I had just been saved from sent a shiver down my spine. I had been close to highly venomous snakes, malaria-carrying mosquitoes, crocodiles, hippos, scorpions and other dangerous creatures on my journey, but it was humans who had almost seen me off.

Whilst we were talking, I checked myself for injuries and found blood on my fingers from a cut above the eye, which must have happened in the initial struggle. My cheeks were hot to the touch and a little swollen from the punches I had received. My neck was sore and stiff when I moved it from side to side and I prayed that no long-term damage had been caused. When I returned to England, an X-ray revealed that there was no fracture, but I needed intensive physiotherapy to unlock the stiffness and put it right.

After about half an hour in the police station, where my

documents were checked and questions were fired at me, the senior officer brought the discussion to a close. Smiling at his colleagues, he uttered a few words, as if to say, 'It was only a bit of fun!' I pointed to the cut above my eye, swollen cheeks, bruised fingers and marks on my wrists.

'Welcome to Mozambique!' I said sarcastically.

The comments were passed to my audience, but I don't think they got the joke. The Comandante asked if I needed to go to the hospital, but I shook my head, telling him that I just needed a wash and get some rest. Besides, I had seen the state of medical facilities along the way and didn't rate my chances in getting any decent help.

Walking out of the station to find somewhere to stay, I noticed how well laid out the town was. The main road was ramrod straight and the minor streets went off it at perfect ninety-degree angles. There were pavements on either side, also straight and, apart from one or two slabs missing, in good condition. Apart from a few clapped-out motorbikes puttering along, there was an absence of cars and as a result the town had a distinctly empty feeling. The only car I saw during my whole time there was the police truck I had arrived in.

Someone had planned this town with care, presumably expecting it to grow in importance, but it seemed to be sliding backwards. There was a small park at an intersection, with benches and what looked like a concrete bandstand in the centre and I wondered how long ago it had seen music. Closer to the Zambezi was an impressive and ornate building with white painted walls and coffee-coloured tiles, and three arches over the main door with a large balcony above. 'Governo Do Districto De Chinde' was painted proudly on the parapet, with the colourful official seal above. Status was obviously important for one who reached the level of Governor, but the building looked so out of place in a town where people lived in huts a few hundred metres away. A grand, equally ornamental church was close by, and I could hear a choir practice taking place, clear voices carrying on the wind.

As I wandered the dusty streets, I reflected again on what had happened, so close to my final destination, where the Zambezi River meets the Indian Ocean. Chinde itself had come to prominence after the Anglo-Portuguese Treaty of 1891, when the British Government was granted a concession to establish a port on a thin sliver of land about the size of a football field to the east of the current town. Outside Portuguese customs control, the port allowed seagoing ships to transfer their cargoes onto river steamers for onward movement up the Zambezi.

The site selected was a sandspit, with a tidal creek virtually separating it from the mainland, making it more of an island than a peninsula. Additional land was granted, inside customs control, to house the slowly growing population of the settlement. The town briefly flourished as the port for British Central Africa, which became Nyasaland (present day Malawi) in 1907, and there were about ten river steamers in operation, transferring goods up the river.

Sadly for Chinde, the port began to be claimed by the sea and was already in decline when a cyclone hit in 1922. The nail in the coffin was when the rail link from Nyasaland to Beira, a port further south, was completed shortly afterwards. The main purpose of the concession had now been removed, the British abandoned the site and the settlement was returned to Portuguese control. Chinde continued to operate as a small port for the export of sugar, but the sun had set on its development and it became very much a backwater, which it has remained to the present day.

I found somewhere to stay on the main street, in spite of having been told there were no hotels. It was a cheap place with no running water like all the others I had stayed in, but it was somewhere to rest and lick my wounds and I was grateful for it.

Sitting on the bed, I noticed the state of my walking shoes, shiny and new six months earlier but now completely destroyed. The hole on the left one had grown larger than a fifty pence coin and there were deep cuts and abrasions on both. They had covered, both on the Camino de Santiago and the Zambezi trek, nearly two thousand kilometres and had served me well.

I took off my shirt and inspected the bruises that had been inflicted a few hours earlier. Gingerly touching the angry looking skin, I noticed three distinct marks on my left side and two on the right and was thankful that my captors hadn't been wearing heavy boots. If they had, I might have had broken ribs to contend with, along with everything else. The bruises on my biceps from being dragged along the track were also profound and tender, the skin already starting to darken. My wrists too were a sorry sight, where the twine used to bind me had dug deeply into the tendons and muscle, the marks showing for weeks afterwards.

As I continued to inspect the marks on my body, I was reminded of David Lemon's journey. As well as catching malaria, on return to the UK he was found to have bilharzia (parasitic flatworms), strongyloides (parasitic roundworms), hydatids (parasitic flatworms) and tick typhus. Somehow, he had made it from the source to the mouth of the Zambezi, which especially at his advanced years was remarkable. Looking down at my stomach, I saw that I was thinner than when I arrived in Africa a few months earlier, but was fairly confident that I hadn't picked up any unwelcome passengers in my system. I learnt later that I had lost a kilo in weight though. A frugal diet and days spent walking long distances had whittled me down to a leaner figure and apart from the physical injuries I felt in good shape.

Once his own expedition had come to an end, David Livingstone described well the effects of a long journey:

'In our case the muscles of the limbs were as hard as boards, and not an ounce of fat existed on any part of the body'. (1)

Chinde. Where the Zambezi River meets the
Indian Ocean and journey's end

Untying the laces and pulling off my shoes, I rolled off
my socks and was pleased to see that my feet were in good
condition. Apart from a little dirt and a scent that is
universally unmistakable, they were ready to go for another
thousand kilometres. My feet had carried me through the
African bush and given me no trouble and I hadn't even had
a single blister, amazing bearing in mind what they had been
through. I felt they deserved some special treatment and,
walking over to the washroom and plastic dustbin full of
water, I sat on a small stool and poured cold water over them
as I massaged the muscles and tendons and cleaned off the
dirt.

Later, after an improvised cold shower and a much-
needed shave, I sauntered slowly through town to where the
Zambezi met the sea. At this point the river was a few
kilometres wide, but it was just one of a number of branches
that meandered through the swamps towards the ocean. The
water flowed gently past, muddy in colour and every so often
I caught sight of a log or large bush floating by. As I looked

east towards the junction of the river and the sea, knowing I had to reach it, I saw tall palm trees lining a ledge along the river beach, their fronds swishing gently in the wind.

On approaching the coast by boat, David Livingstone had described what he saw:

'The coast is low and covered with mangrove swamps, among which are sandy patches clothed with grass, creeping plants and stunted palms. The land trends nearly east and west, without any notable feature to guide the navigator, and it is difficult to make out the river's mouth…' (1)

Walking past fishermen's huts of wood and mud in the shadow of swaying palms, I left habitation a few kilometres behind me and made my way along narrow sandy paths and around fields. Cutting through some thick vegetation, I rounded a corner and saw a young woman walking towards me, weighed down by a heavy load of wood balanced on her head. Her brain was obviously concentrating hard on what she was doing and it took a while for her eyes to lift up to mine. When they did, the look of shock on her face was frightening and I forced a smile to try to assure her that I wasn't a threat. In a split second, she raised her arms to her head, pushed her load to the ground and ran off back to the town, wailing in horror.

'For God's sake!' I shouted irritably.

My nerves were jangled and I had visions of a mob racing out of the trees to teach me another lesson. I had definitely had enough drama for one day. Moving swiftly on, I put some distance between me and the unfortunate encounter.

Checking my satnav, the path continued to take me parallel with the beach and not towards it, but I continued on in the hope of reaching the sea. After another kilometre following a barrier of mangroves, I was still no closer to the beach and watched the path continue to follow the line of the coast as I heard the faint sound of the surf in the distance. I was hot, frustrated and fed up and wanted my journey to be over.

Taking a path through the mangroves, I had to wade

through murky knee-deep water which smelt of rotten eggs due to the oxygen-poor, sulphuric nature of the coastal ecosystem. On areas of exposed sand, palm-sized crabs scuttled back into their holes on my approach. On some of the thicker branches, barnacles had taken hold and I had to take care in placing my hands for fear of cutting my skin.

Stepping out of the fetid water, I made solid ground again and was grateful for the smell of the sea. I strolled across the sandy beach and eventually stood facing the water. Walking slowly towards it, I let out a long sigh, the relief of finally making it washing over me. The waves lapped gently against the shoreline and the harsh sunlight made the water dazzle. For a month I had imagined racing into the ocean and swimming in salt water for the first time in the country, but I just stood there motionless, reflecting on the journey.

I had walked nearly nine hundred kilometres in thirty-four days, most of it solo, following the Zambezi River across Mozambique. I had experienced exceptional kindness from strangers, but also been jostled, harassed, chased and beaten. Seeing wondrous scenery, I had waded through rivers and trekked across a great variety of terrain. I had come close, probably too close, to some of Africa's wildest beasts and had been thrilled with the encounters. I had memories to last a lifetime.

I should have been elated; I had walked all along the north shore of the Zambezi where the present-day Lake Cahora Bassa sits, which hadn't been done since David Livingstone's time over a hundred and fifty years before. But I felt flat. After the experiences of the morning, where I had come close to being killed by a mob, I was ready to return to my own world. I had stepped into darkness and needed to make my way back to the light.

Epilogue

It took over two days, travelling day and night and using a variety of transport, to cover the four hundred kilometres back to Tete. The saga began when I dropped into the police station on my way back from the beach and asked one of the officers who spoke a little English, what the best way out of the delta was. I had looked at it when researching the trip, but there was no obvious way and I had decided to worry about my exit plan when I was actually in Chinde.

'It's all arranged!' smiled the officer.

'What do you mean?' I replied in disbelief. 'What's arranged?'

'We have a boat, leaving at midnight.'

I made the assumption that they had access to a police boat, which turned out to be wildly optimistic.

It turned out that the Comandante was feeling sorry for me and had asked the officer to take some leave and escort me back to civilisation. We would take a boat back to Luabo and then make our way to Quelimane, the regional capital further up the coast. It was a huge dog-leg route, but I put my doubts to one side, trusting the local knowledge of my hosts. No doubt they wanted rid of me, but I was grateful for the help and was told to report back at ten that evening.

Returning to my room, I tried to take a nap to catch up on lost sleep, but found it difficult due to the harrowing events of the morning. Everything that had happened raced through my mind in minute detail like a whirlwind and I couldn't find the switch to make it go away and allow me to fall asleep.

Later, I had some food where I was staying and made the preparations for my departure. Walking over to the police station at the agreed time, I sat with some officers on benches overlooking the square. They watched with interest as locals went about town, occasionally calling out to girls who shyly looked back.

It was a Friday and a sense of celebration was in the air,

no doubt after a hard-working week. Some music was playing to our left in what looked like the local bar, but in reality was just a shop selling beer with a few chairs outside. Later in the evening, figures staggered around in the darkness, obviously the worse for drink, and one man even slumped on the ground behind us, much to the amusement of the officers.

Finally, after it had passed eleven, it was time to go and I strolled down towards the river with the officer. I asked him to remind me what route we were taking, but all he said was 'Quelimane. You take bus from there.' I knew that it was a fair way north and well out of my way, but didn't argue as I was just pleased to be leaving. Walking through dark and semi-deserted streets, we eventually arrived at a beach on the river and the policeman strolled over to some figures taking warmth from a fire.

Returning, he led me down in virtual darkness to the boat, similar to the one I had used a few days earlier. Throwing our bags over the gunwale, we hauled ourselves up the side, stepped over some rails and into the main section. It was beached in the mud at a precipitous angle and wasn't going anywhere fast and the idea of a swift escape from the town quickly disappeared. Some people had already spread themselves out on the floor, covering themselves with blankets, and it was difficult to avoid stepping on them. The only space available were on planks running across the boat and I wedged myself in next to crates of empty beer bottles and tried to sleep. The smell of stale beer around me was awful and stuck in my nostrils for the entire voyage.

At around two in the morning I woke from my doze to the sound of agitated voices beside the boat. Peering over the side, I could just make out the water lapping against the vessel and knew that the tide had turned. The men were pushing the boat away from the beach. They seemed to be taking a huge risk with the water above their knees in a crocodile-infested river, but I was grateful for their efforts.

Eventually, we were prised from the mud like a cork from

a bottle, as the water took our weight and the engine fired into life. Pointing westwards, we began to chug along the river as the passengers tried to catch more sleep and I gave a silent prayer for being able to finally leave Chinde. It was bitterly cold and despite pulling on my fleece and pulling the liner up to my chest, I couldn't settle and longed for the first rays of sun. After an hour or so, I nodded off on my cramped perch and didn't wake up until we were nearly there. Checking my satnav, I saw that Luabo was close and enjoyed the views along the river, slowly coming to life.

When we pulled up at the beach, there was a scramble to get off as everyone was desperate to stretch their limbs after an uncomfortable journey. It had taken over five hours to travel the thirty kilometres.

We wandered the few last kilometres to Luabo as the light intensified, past shops and stalls that were being prepared for the day, and headed towards the track that I had been on a few days earlier. There were a few motorbike taxis parked under some trees and after some negotiation, the policeman and I climbed onto the bike. I shook my head as we raced off towards Mopeia, amazed at the risks people took to get around the country. There were three of us on a 50cc machine, where only the rider had a helmet. I wasn't sure how many motorbike deaths there were every year in Mozambique, but I held on for dear life.

After an uncomfortable few hours of bumping along the track, we arrived at Mopeia and made our way to the minibus stop. People were bustling around, forcing themselves and their belongings onto vehicles, and I anticipated another ordeal of a journey ahead. Buying some fritters to share with the policeman, we then wedged ourselves into our seats and trundled towards Quelimane. We made random stops along the way and gradually the minibus emptied and I was glad to see the outskirts of the city, five hours after leaving Mopeia.

Quelimane is a seaport and the administrative capital of Zambezia province, with a population of two hundred thousand. Boasting a large hospital, a small airport, a few cathedrals, a mosque and a university, it is the fourth largest city in Mozambique. It was founded by Muslim slave traders, who used it as a base to ship their cargo from Central Africa across to the Middle East. The famous Portuguese explorer Vasco da Gama visited the town in 1498 on his travels along the coast, but fell out with its inhabitants and had to flee for fear of attack. During the Portuguese colonial era, the town's infrastructure was improved and it was used as a trading station, mainly for the export of tea, cotton, sugar cane and coconuts.

David Livingstone, who also visited the town, referred to the low, muddy, fever-haunted and mosquito-swarming site as unsuitable for normal habitation. He was probably right. It was a scruffy place, with litter alongside the road and the buildings in poor repair. As we walked to the main bus station, the policeman who had accompanied me asked if I could buy his ticket to Maputo, a thousand miles away. He told me it was where his family lived and he was looking forward to seeing them. As I had already paid for most of his transport, I declined his request, which surprised him.

'But you have money and I have looked after you during the journey,' he said.

'I'm grateful for your help, but you need to get your own ticket,' I replied.

He asked a few more times, but once he knew my mind was made up, he wandered off and I never saw him again. At the station, I asked for the best way to Tete and was told I had to go via Chimoio, a long way south. I was pleased that I had secured a ticket but not so pleased that it left at four in the morning, some twelve hours away.

Spotting a Bangladeshi restaurant across the road, I headed towards it, suddenly feeling hungry. I hadn't eaten in such a long time and wondered what was in store. There was warm chicken and rice, which could have been better, but it also had Wi-Fi and I was able to let my loved ones know that I was safe. Phone reception and access to the internet had been non-existent for the past week.

227

I contacted Chaz to see how he had fared and was pleased to hear that he had also completed the journey, having arrived in Chinde a few days before me. I told him about my ordeal at the hands of the villagers and he was shocked, saying that I had been lucky. Somehow, he had dodged the crazed villagers on the island but had experienced his own problems with the locals earlier in his journey near Tete, when he had been locked up for a few days trying to pass through a village. Apparently, they were suspicious of his being there and he only managed to get away when his captors let him out to go to the toilet. I thought back to the time when we had split up near the lake and I knew that we would have been better off staying together. We now had different journeys to remember, but we had both suffered for that moment of rashness. Like me, Chaz hadn't hung around Chinde for long but had travelled south to Beira before flying out.

As I was casually catching up with world news on my phone, I was appalled to see stories about Islamic violence in Mozambique, north of where I was sitting. Militants had been raiding villages and police stations and carrying out unspeakable atrocities and I was so glad to be leaving the region that very night. Scrolling down a BBC article entitled 'Mozambique jihadists behead villagers', I was aghast to learn that at least ten people had been beheaded in recent days by suspected militants. Children were reported to be amongst those targeted in the attack on Monjane village in Cabo Delgado province. The article went on to explain that an Islamist militant group had carried out sporadic attacks in the region in 2017 and were known locally as al-Shabab, but it had no known links to the Somali jihadist group of the same name.

I was hoping that the restaurant would stay open till late, as the city had an edgy feel to it, with strange characters lurking in the darkness. Sadly, it closed at ten and I had to stay awake and make myself comfortable on the concrete bus station floor, along with the other passengers.

Later, when I was stretching my legs by the entrance, a

fight broke out and a local man was hit on the head with a bottle. Blood was splattered on the floor and the man stumbled around for a few minutes, looking for the bathroom and sobbing in agony. Someone gave him some cloths and he cleaned himself up as best he could and staggered off down the street. When I returned to my spot on the floor, there was a trail of gore across the forecourt.

It was a long night, as if time had stood still, but eventually the bus arrived and we set off across the country to Chimoio. It was a bumpy ride and took all day and we arrived as the light was starting to fade. We passed through numerous military checkpoints on the journey and whenever my face was spotted, a soldier would usually wander over to me and ask where I was going. They were friendly enough, but obviously surprised to see a lone white man so far from home.

Chimoio was a bustling, rundown place, a key staging point for people travelling from north to south. Jumping out of the minibus, I asked the driver where I could connect to Tete and he shrugged his shoulders, telling me that nothing would leave before the morning. I didn't relish the opportunity of experiencing another night in a Mozambican bus station and asked around if there were other options. It turned out there was a lorry park out of town that locals used to complete their journeys and taking the risk, I headed out to find it.

Arriving at the place, I found lorries scattered around a dusty piece of land, some with lights on inside, but many blacked out and dark. Most of the vehicles looked as though their work had been done for the day and I didn't rate my chances in securing a lift. Knowing that it was probably going to be another long night, I wandered over to a petrol station and bought some supplies to sustain me.

As I walked back to the lorry park, I noticed some vehicles parked on the road and approached a few drivers to see if they were going to Tete, four hundred kilometres away. Most were only going short distances, but the driver at the end of the line told me he was going there and agreed to take me.

After a long journey through the night, we arrived on the outskirts of Tete, crossing over the new bridge that I had seen a few weeks before. I was exhausted, having not slept properly for a few days and was glad to have finally arrived. Paying the driver a nominal amount, I wandered over to a coffee shop and settled in a chair, shaded by the early morning sun.

Relishing a fresh coffee, something I hadn't had in weeks, I felt relaxed for the first time in days and allowed my eyes to close for a moment, knowing I was safe. I reflected again on my journey along the Zambezi, as locals prepared themselves for the new day, and shook my head slowly at some of the memories. It had been a tough experience and my time in Mozambique had taught me that the country, whilst having many attractions, was definitely not for beginners.

Shortly after returning to the UK, I began to research the vampire myths in East Africa and was shocked to find a BBC article entitled 'Malawi curfew over 'vampire' killings'. Intrigued, I learnt that at least five people had been killed in southern Malawi when I had been nearing the coast, after they had been accused of behaving like vampires. According to reports, the victims were killed by vigilante mobs who suspected them of drinking human blood as part of magic rituals and a night-time curfew had been imposed by the government to prevent any more deaths. The article highlighted a UN report suggesting that the vampirism rumours had originated from Mozambique, and spread across the border to a few southern Malawian districts. It was unclear what had sparked the fears, but villagers had apparently set up road blocks as they tried to hunt the 'vampires' down.

I was lucky to get out of there in one piece.

Bibliography

Most of the material for this book came from my diaries and photographs which recorded events during the journey. Additional information, to add further texture, was taken from the following publications:

(1)   Narrative of an Expedition to the Zambesi and its Tributaries, 1858-1864, by David and Charles Livingstone. 2001. Gerald Duckworth and Co. First published in 1865 by John Murray, London.

(2)   Livingstone's River. A History of the Zambezi Expedition, 1858-1864 by George Martelli. 1970. Published by Chatto & Windus, London.

(3)   In Livingstone's Footsteps. Walking the Mighty Zambezi, by David Lemon. 2016. Independently published.

Lightning Source UK Ltd.
Milton Keynes UK
UKHW040731151122
412232UK00007B/413